BELOVED
DAUGHTERS

BELOVED DAUGHTERS

100 YEARS OF PAPAL TEACHING ON WOMEN

RICHARD LEONARD SJ

Foreword by Elizabeth Johnson CSJ

David Lovell Publishing
Melbourne Australia

First published in 1995 and reissued in 2018 by
David Lovell Publishing
PO Box 44, Kew East
Victoria 3102 Australia
tel/fax +61 3 9859 0000
email publisher@davidlovellpublishing.com

Front cover: 'Annunciation', oil on paper by Charles Watt, from an original work by Rien Poortvliet, in *Hij was een van ons*, 1974
Design by David Lovell Publishing
Typeset in 12/16 Perpetua
This edition printed through Ingram Spark

National Library of Australia Cataloguing-in-Publication data

Leonard, Richard, 1963 - .
Beloved daughters : 100 years of papal teaching on women.

Bibliography
Includes index
ISBN: 978 1 86355 045 1 (paperback)
1. Fiorenza, Elisabeth Schüssler, 1938 – . 2. Catholic Church – Doctrines. 3. Women in the Catholic Church. 4. Popes – Teaching office – History. I. Title.
282.082

Acknowledgements
This book has its origins in a Master of Theology thesis. I owe a great deal to Rev. Dr Andrew Hamilton SJ for his encouragement, patience and theological insight throughout the duration of the project. I am also grateful to Dr Elaine Wainwright RSM, Dr Brendan Byrne SJ, Rev. Prof. Dorothy Lee, Fr Brian Moore SJ, and Mr Simon Pincus, who at various stages gave me important criticisms and advice.

I would also like to pay tribute to the Jesuit communities at Campion and Xavier Colleges, Melbourne, for their support and assistance. Finally, I would like to express my appreciation for the help I have received from the teaching staff at the United Faculty of Theology, Parkville, the Melbourne College of Divinity, and in particular Dr Lawrence McIntosh of the Joint Theological Library, Parkville, Melbourne.

To my family:
Joan, Tracey, Peter
Michelle, Amy, Thomas
and Emily

Foreword

Elizabeth A. Johnson csj*

FOR MANY WOMEN in the church who dream of equality and full participation, one of the best texts of Vatican II is article 29 of *Gaudium et spes*, the Constitution on the Church in the Modern World. Speaking of the ideal for human community, this passage asserts the fundamental equality of all human persons insofar as all are created in the image of God, redeemed by Christ and destined for glory. True, the bishops go on, everyone is not alike from the point of view of intellectual and physical gifts, which differ. But then comes a resounding affirmation:

> Nevertheless, with respect to the fundamental rights of the person, every type of discrimination, whether social or cultural, whether based on sex, race, colour, social condition, language or religion, is to be overcome and eradicated as contrary to God's intent.

We note today that the theological term for what is contrary to God's intent is 'sin'. Thus the Second Vatican Council taught that bias against women on the basis of their sex is sinful. The text itself

---

*Elizabeth Johnson csj is a Distinguished Professor of Theology at Fordham University, New York. She is considered one of the leading systematic theologians in the English-speaking world and lectures widely to church and academic assemblies at home and abroad. One of her best known books is *She Who Is: The Mystery of God in Feminist Theological Discourse* (1992), and other books include *Ask the Beasts: Darwin and the Love of God* (2014), *Quest for the Living God* (2007), *Truly Our Sister: A Theology of Mary in the Communion of Saints* (2003), *The Church Women Want* (2002), and *Consider Jesus: Waves of Renewal in Christology* (1990).

leaves no doubt that this interpretation was in the bishops' mind, for the passage continues:

> For in truth it must still be regretted that fundamental personal rights are not yet being universally honored. Such is the case of a woman who is denied the right and freedom to choose a husband, to embrace a state of life, or to acquire an education or cultural benefits equal to those recognized for men.

On the one hand, the church teaches that it is wrong to deny women the right and freedom to embrace a state of life. On the other hand, the same church bars women from embracing the state of life which is ordained priesthood. What is the source of this inconsistency?

The bedrock on which the role of women stands or falls, and therefore the battlefield for issues of equality, is theological anthropology, namely, the assessment of what a person is before God, through Christ, in the power of the Spirit. Currently there are two differing anthropologies in conflict on this point. One, promoted by women theologians, is a holistic anthropology of equivalence and partnership in which sexual difference does not become the sole marker of identity but rather combines in myriad ways with race, class, ethnic, historical, geographic and cultural differences to define each person as unique. In this view, the diversity of personal characteristics and gifts is not predetermined by sex but ranges across a wide spectrum for both women and men.

The other theological anthropology, promoted by thinkers who would preserve the custom of male rule, is a dualistic anthropology of complementarity in which sexual difference becomes elevated to an ontological norm dividing human beings into two separate types. Women are cast as polar opposites to men and the differences between them are maximized. 'Masculine nature', with its orientation to rationality, order and decision-making, is equipped for leadership in the public realm. 'Feminine nature', with its orientation to love, life and nurturing, is fit for the private domain of childbearing, homemaking and care for the vulnerable. With its roots in Hellenistic philosophy that equated the male principle with spirit and the female principle with matter, prizing the former over the latter, this system of gender dualism generally issues in subordination for women. Furthermore, so-called masculine and feminine traits and roles are rigidly assigned so that a woman seeking a public role is said to be acting against her own nature.

The teaching of the papacy about women has generally fallen into the anthropology of complementarity type. It is the merit of this book that it traces for all to see the development of papal teaching over the last century up to its current promise and ambiguity. There has been real advance from the classical tradition where women were denied equality of nature and the dignity of being created in the image of God in their own right. Instead, Pope John Paul II emphatically affirms that women and men are equal in their human dignity, both having rational minds and free will and both equally created in the image and likeness of God. Furthermore, though holding fast to the distinctive qualities of women's nature, the pope insists that these be equally valued rather than seen as inferior, buttressing their significance with appeal to the model of the Virgin Mary, Mother of God.

The limits of the dualistic model, however, prevent this newly retrieved teaching on equality of nature from being applied to equality of social roles. Instead, women are identified with their reproductive function, praised as virgins and mothers, and cautioned about losing their femininity in the search for equality. What results is a kind of romantic feminism – women are so ordered to love that they are almost too good to get involved in the messiness of the public realm.

Many women respond as did one of my college students in a paper on *Mulieris dignitatem*: 'As a young women of the late twentieth century, do I want to be so highly exalted? No, I would rather be equal.' The point being, of course, that by boxing women's identity into a narrow range of gender stereotypes, a dualistic anthropology inevitably privileges men in terms of psychological and political power.

Papal teaching now affirms the equality of women and men by nature in creation and by grace in Christ. In doing so it departs from centuries of theological tradition. At the same time it asserts an essential difference between women and men that mandates separate social roles and thereby inequality in practice. Is there need to depart here also from dualistic tradition? To put the question most sharply: Is the idea of women's 'special nature' according to the intention of God made known in compassionate, liberating ministry of Jesus Christ? Or is this an example (however unintentional) of discrimination on the basis of sex and thus contrary to God's intent?

This book performs a real service in providing access to some of the primary material necessary for intelligent participation in this conversation.

Contents

Preface

MANY WOMEN AND MEN are surprised to hear that I have been studying feminist theology for some years now. After this initial surprise comes either suspicion at my motives or congratulations.

One of the most important things this study has taught me is that no one comes to theology value-neutral. We all bring our personal history, political and social agendas, ecclesiastical perspectives and experience of God. Feminist theology has encouraged writers to declare what these influences are, so that readers have an opportunity to understand the position from which the writer writes.

It is not by accident that I have been attracted to the feminist critical school in theology over recent years. When I reflect on my own history I can begin to see the influence that strong, independent women have had on my life.

My father died suddenly when I was two years of age. My mother was thirty-two years old and she had three children under seven and a portfolio of business interests to manage and direct. Except for the child rearing, she had little experience and even less interest in these tasks. At no stage, as I was growing up, can I ever remember my mother feeling as though she was not up to the task because of her gender. While she often felt that her nursing education and socialization as a 'young Catholic lady' were inadequate for the task of heading up a business empire, being a woman in itself presented no obstacle.

The first five years of my primary school education were overseen by women. Most of these women were Irish Sisters of Mercy, or Australians deeply steeped in this tradition. They had such engaging names as Sr M. Consuelo, Sr M. Wenceslaus, Sr M. Terence and Sr M. Leo. I seem to be luckier than some others who came through a similar period of Catholic education. These women were good teachers, demanding but fair disciplinarians; they encouraged us to think for ourselves, care for those in need and make a positive contribution to the church and the nation. There would have been 500 children in St Saviour's Primary School in 1968, and it was completely run by women. Grade Six was a big shock to my system at the Irish Christian Brother's Junior School.

Many other women have been present in my life in ordinary and extraordinary ways since I left St Saviour's: girlfriends, teachers, lecturers, colleagues, house sharers, fellow students, domestic staff, surrogate grandmothers and mothers, secretaries, retreat guides and spiritual directors. However the one that stands out for me is my sister, Tracey. Since her car accident in my second year noviceship, I have seen how a woman can pick up the pieces of a broken life from the ruins of a broken body and decide to live, when death would be so much easier for everyone. I have also seen through Tracey how women care for each other and completely reorganize their lives so that they can respond adequately to the tragedy present. The women in Tracey's life, and Tracey herself, refuse to be mastered or driven by suffering and pain.

These are the models of womanhood that I had with me when I came to theologize. These women will not be limited by social mores and education, institutional demands and expectations, or by the pain and suffering of tragedy. These women were also my first teachers in faith, my earliest role models for what it means and costs to believe, and today are an ideal of how one can confront the face of evil and still hold to God.

I have found it relatively easy to embrace the concerns of the feminist school, not only because I had never known or been educated to believe that women were to be excluded from certain religious areas because of their gender, but because I have been the recipient of the Divine through their words and witness. This is not to exclude men. I have experienced God through men as well and this is precisely the point: the rise of the feminist school can afford the Christian community the opportunity to reconcile the male/female dichotomy that so infuses and limits our understanding of God, Christ, church and ourselves.

My experience has been such that the aspirations of women in the church do not mean that they have to be bad news for men. Accordingly, when I came to write a thesis in this area, some years ago, I was conscious of trying to further the communication between women and men in theology. As a result I chose to write on men who have written on women. It is my hope that the fruit of this research and reflection is helpful for the life of our community of faith.

Introduction

Reading Papal Teaching

FOR MOST PEOPLE papal teaching is a maze. The language is complex, the style foreign and the agenda obscure. This maze can be so confusing that many people give up on it. But they do not have to, if only they arm themselves with a few basic tools.

Before we look at the papal documents concerning women over the last 100 years, it is necessary to understand how to read them.

Not all documents from Rome carry the same weight. Not all documents are intended for everyone in the church and the world. Whether the declaration is a legal or teaching document, whether it has come from the office of the pope or from a Vatican department, these distinctions matter. Too often people quote from papal statements as though they all have the same authority. Balcony speeches and encyclicals are used without reference to their status. The fact is that no matter how much I may like what a particular pope has said in a speech from his study, it does not make the same demands on the Catholic community that a formally promulgated declaration does. The Vatican understands this and continues to use a modified system of teaching hierarchy handed down over the centuries.

Intelligent readers of papal teaching are prepared; they know the moves before they go on to the field.

Papal pronouncements

There are seven types of pronouncements that a pope in the Roman Catholic Church can publish in his own right and in his own name.[1] These fall into two categories. The first concerns the legal life of the church and the second concerns the teaching life of the church.

When the pope is acting as legislator for the Catholic community he can issue three types of documents. The most authoritative is an Apostolic Constitution. Such a document deals with the most serious doctrinal or disciplinary matters. It is usually released at a liturgical ritual designed to focus the attention of the whole church on its statements. It can be an infallible declaration, but is not by definition so. The most recent apostolic constitution which was defined as infallible was *Munificentissimus Deus* of Pope Pius XII in 1950. This document solemnly defined Mary's assumption into heaven as a dogma of Catholic faith. An apostolic constitution which is not infallible is John Paul II's *Fidei depositium* on the publication of *The Catechism of the Catholic Church* in 1992.

The second level of legal papal pronouncement in is a *Motu Proprio*. This document is an executive declaration that establishes a new law, confirms an existing custom or directs action on a disciplinary matter. It is strictly a legislative document from the pope's own hand, concerning internal legal matters. In recent years this form of papal decree has most commonly been used to establish bodies

---

1. For a full discussion of this topic see R. Brown, 'Bishops and theologians: "dispute" surrounded by fiction', *Origins*, 7 (1978), pp. 675-682; J. T. Catoir, 'Papal Documents, in *The Catholic Encyclopedia*, vol. 4, 1967, pp. 946-947; A. Dulles, 'What is magisterium?', *Origins*, 6 (1976), pp. 81-87; F. Morrisey, 'Papal and curial pronouncements: their canonical significance in the light of the 1983 Code of Canon Law', *The Jurist*, 50 (1990), pp. 102-125; K. Rahner & J. Ratzinger, *The Episcopate and the Primacy*, New York: Orbis, 1962; G. Weigel, 'The significance of papal pronouncements', *The Papal Encyclicals in Their Historical Context*, ed. A. Fremantle, New York, 1956.

for the authentic interpretation of the teachings of ecumenical councils or the Code of Canon Law. While it can be issued to the whole church and is published for them to read, it is usually directed to the relevant group or person who has responsibility for that area in the life of the church.

The third level of pronouncement a pope issues as legislator is that of a Decretal Letter. Over the last twenty years this letter has been used exclusively in proclaiming a person's canonization. While this document calls for the assent of the faithful, there is 'some dispute among theologians as to the invoking of infallibility with this proclamation.'[2]

When the pope is acting as Teacher for the Catholic Church he can issue four types of teaching. The first level of papal pronouncement in this category is an Encyclical Letter. This declaration deals with doctrinal, social or moral issues that are relevant to life of the Universal Church at a given time. Since the pontificate of John XXIII (1958-1962), encyclical letters have been addressed to all people 'of good will'. They are authoritative teaching of the highest order, but are not of themselves infallible. These letters are part of the ordinary teaching of the church and serve to clarify points of doctrine or to give counsel on important social and moral issues. Still, Catholics are obliged, unless for serious reasons of informed and sincerely held conscience, to assent to the teaching encyclical letters outline.

The second level is an Apostolic Letter. This document is addressed to either particular groups or to the whole church. It is usually published to mark a significant moment in the church's life. When the pope issues an apostolic letter it is in his role as teacher and pastor. He does not have to consult the world's bishops before

---

2. Morrisey, F., 'Papal and curial pronouncements', p. 104.

issuing this teaching. Hence such letters normally outline the pope's thinking on significant theological issues of moment and give suggestions and directions for the conduct of the life of the church. While an apostolic letter is not an infallible document, and does not make the same claim to assent as an encyclical, it is an authoritative declaration. This requires that the people of the church pay close attention to the mind of the pope on the issue on which he expounds. An apostolic letter communicates to Catholics the pope's current thinking on an issue and, if relevant, enables them to make an informed decision of conscience.

The third level of papal pronouncement is an Apostolic Exhortation. Unlike an encyclical letter, this declaration is addressed to particular groups, often 'all bishops in peace and communion with the Apostolic See'. It is primarily an exposition by the pope on a point of devotion, an article of faith or to mark a special occasion. While the content of this document is usually published for everyone to read, it is primarily intended to, literally, exhort bishops or individuals throughout the church to give special attention to the matter dealt with in the declaration in their own diocese or area of responsibility.

The final form a papal teaching statement can take is that of an Allocution. An allocution takes a variety of forms: homilies, press releases, speeches, diplomatic addresses and public messages. These documents are personal pronouncements of explanation. They carry no demands on Catholics to adhere to the teaching contained therein, but reveal the mind of the Bishop of Rome, in his role as chief pastor and teacher of the church.

Documents on women

This very brief survey of the terrain of papal teaching enable us to move to the documents themselves. It often comes as a surprise to many people that popes over the last 100 years have spoken directly about or to women over forty times. Most of these reflections have taken the form of papal allocutions. They were addressed to specific groups of women, both religious and lay on an issue of immediate concern to them.[3]

For our purposes, I have taken what I judge to be the most important statements about women from the popes in the last 100 years. The criteria for selection? My starting point is the universal application of the content of the teaching and the higher level of authority of the teaching itself. Thus numerous statements at the allocution level are not included in this study.

As well as looking at papal declarations, I believe it is essential to look at the teaching of the Second Vatican Council and the work of two Vatican departments: the Commission for the Role of Women in the Church and Society [1973-76] and the Congregation for the Doctrine of the Faith. While the documents from these sources are not papal pronouncements, they were promulgated as church teaching under the name and authority of Paul VI and have had an enormous impact on the thinking of the John Paul II. An important example is the 'Declaration on certain questions regarding the admission of women to the ministerial priesthood' (1977) from the Congregation for the Doctrine of the Faith. For clarity and context, they must be included. I will nominate the level of authority these documents have when we deal with them.

I will look at each pope since Leo XIII (1878-1903) and take a selection of his specific teaching on women. My thesis is that from Leo XIII to Paul VI there were two separate areas of papal pronouncements that focused on women in particular: mariological teaching, that is, teaching about Mary, and social teaching. These areas were

---

3. For an edited anthology of papal speeches about women, without commentary or comment, from Leo XIII to Pius XII, see *Women in the Church and the World*, published by the Monks of Solesmes, 1958.

kept quite distinct. However, in the teaching of Pope John Paul II, particularly in the apostolic letter *Mulieris dignitatem*, they have been fused together.

A word about terms: by mariological teaching, I mean papal pronouncements on Mary; by social teaching I mean papal pronouncements on Catholic social doctrine. However, under the banner of social teaching, I will also include the moral teaching of Pius XI and Pius XII. I do this because it was in the context of moral development, marriage and personal formation that both these popes dealt with women's issues in any detail. It will be necessary, also, when dealing with Pius XII, to look at documents that are not encyclicals. Most of Pius XII's teaching on the role of women came in the form of addresses to various women's groups.

This book, then, will survey chronologically the social and then the mariological teachings of the popes from Leo XIII to John Paul II. This overview will highlight the development in thought and change of direction in papal reflections on the dignity and vocation of women in each area. Why start with Leo? First, because the scope of this book could not accommodate a full historical analysis of papal decrees previous to Leo. Second, because the issue of women's rights and participation in social and political life came to the fore in the 1890s, arguably the beginning of the modern period; consequently, the church has very little specific response to the status of women up to that point. Third, Leo's pontificate, mainly through his social teaching, ushered in a new era in official Catholic thought, which successive popes have built on, developed and clarified.

Key Themes

Several themes recur in the social teaching of the church in regard to women. They include the points that women should not be exploited in the workplace, by political systems, or in the home. Women have special status because of their feminine nature and that their appropriate roles are as homemaker, wife and mother. Virginity in the consecrated life is the highest calling that a woman can pursue. Any abuse of women by their husbands or society is to be condemned. All these facets of the church's social doctrine are accepted and developed in the teachings of all the popes.

However, there are also a number of areas where the present papal teaching moves in new directions, in contrast to earlier pronouncements on women. The first is the support and praise of women who enter into public and political life, as a sign of the times. The second is that special attention is due to women who are single and yet not in the consecrated life. Interestingly, John Paul II argues that women are essentially equal to men in dignity and yet through their vocation as virgins and mothers they are called to higher things. Consequently, he restates the church's position against women lowering themselves to become priests in his most recent apostolic letter, *Ordinatio sacerdotalis*.

In terms of mariology, it is clear that most of the traditional teaching about Mary and women has revolved around Mary as model. The popes up to Paul VI consistently taught that Mary is the model virgin and mother for women. She is also the model of true discipleship and virginity for all people.

Importantly, Paul VI moved the focus to Jesus as the person whom Christians should imitate, and Mary was held up as an outstanding example of this choice. John Paul II in *Mulieris dignitatem* however, returns to the earlier papal teaching about Mary as exemplar of virginity, motherhood and femininity in general. In fact, Mary, through the incarnation, becomes the ultimate example of Christian womanhood, and the veneration paid to her in the church becomes the model for the way society should esteem all women.

Part 1

From Rerum novarum *up to* Mulieris dignitatem

Chapter 1

Women in Catholic Social Teaching

BY 1891, A MAJOR SOCIAL upheaval had gripped industrialized Europe, especially Britain and Germany. The rapid technological developments of the nineteenth century meant that higher productivity from workers was demanded, so that company owners could make greater profits. This led to outrageous working conditions, low rates of pay, exploitation of women and children in the labour market and extreme poverty. Out of this context, Leo XIII (1878–1903) wrote an encyclical, *Rerum novarum* ('On the Condition of Labour'). Leo included two general statements in his teaching that had direct relevance to the women who, in 1891, made up a large section of the work force. In section 26, he says that, although people have differing gifts and talents, God has granted to each woman and man equal dignity, and this must be respected. Later, he lays down as a guiding principle for social development the right of all people to participate in society. However, women's participation was seen in terms of the home: 'a women is by nature fitted for home work, and it is that which is best adapted at once to preserve her modesty and to promote the good bringing up of children and the well being of the family.'[4]

---

4. Camp, R., 'From passive submission to complementary partnership: the papal conception of a women's place in church and society since 1878', *The Catholic Historical Review*, 76, 3 (1990), p. 510.

Pius X (1903–1914) made only one unofficial pronouncement in which he directly refers to, or appeals to, women. He never wrote a universal social encyclical. In fact Pius X 'spoke rarely on social problems and made little original contribution when he did'.[5] In the only recorded speech this pope made about women, he said, 'There is much to admire in the feminist desire to elevate women intellectually and socially, but the Lord protect us from political feminism.'[6]

World War I and its aftermath preoccupied Benedict XV's (1914–1922) entire time and energy during office. He too never wrote a social encyclical, and of the twelve encyclicals he did write seven were devoted to the war and a call for peace. Benedict did, however, restate Leo XIII's views on women's domestic responsibilities. He argued that women were in occupations 'ill befitting their sex', and others 'abandoned the duties of house wife for which they were fashioned, to cast themselves recklessly into the current of life'.[7]

Pius XI (1922 –1939) spoke directly about women three times in his encyclicals. *Casti connubii* ('On Chaste Wedlock') was published on 31 December 1930 as a response to 'the present conditions, needs, errors and vices that affect the family and society'. This letter was wide ranging in its interests, moving from the reason for and theology of marriage, to condemning modern fallacies regarding marriage (for example, de facto relationships, birth control, abortion, sterilization, adultery and divorce), to remedies for the current crisis of belief in the church's law regarding marriage.

In section 74, Pius XI writes that one of the modern errors that needs to be corrected is the challenge to 'the honourable and trust-

---

5. Camp, R., *The papal ideology of social reform*, Leiden: Brill, 1969, p. 14.
6. Quoted in Camp, R., 'From passive submission ...', p. 512.
7. See Camp, R., 'From passive submission ...', p. 512.

ing obedience which the woman owes to the man. Many of them [feminists] even go further and assert that such a subjection of one party to the other is unworthy of human dignity, that the rights of husband and wife are equal.' Pius XI did not agree with this view of women's liberation at all, but saw this attitude as a dangerous 'debasing' of the 'rational and exalted liberty which belongs to the noble office of a Christian woman and wife'. It is not that the woman should be 'raised' to the status of men, but 'if the woman descends from her truly regal throne ... she debases her womanly character and the dignity of motherhood'. This exalted vocation of wife and mother is hers as a result of 'the natural disposition and temperament of the female sex'.

Quadragesimo anno ('The Reconstruction of the Social Order') was an encyclical written in the midst of the great economic depression of the 1930s. Pius XI teaches in this letter that the moral law's implications for the social and economic crisis confronting the world lead the church to criticize both capitalism and communism. He defends the rights of workers and those in poverty and pleads for workers, employers, governments and other organizations to establish a more just and equitable social order.

Because social reconstruction should protect the rights and dignity of the poor, he says, families have a pre-eminent claim on the resources of society and that just wages are their due. In fact, Pius XI is the first pope to give unqualified support to the principle of a 'family wage'. He believed that until this wage is in place universally 'women and children should not in any way be abused by those who control the means of production'.

Pius XI, then, holds two major focuses in tension with regard to women: the rights and dignity of those oppressed by employers, and concern at women asserting control over their own lives, bodies and marriages. However, he also earnestly desired lay women to be involved in 'Catholic-action'[8] and encouraged women to be active in social movements

Pius XII (1939 –1958) presents particular problems in relation to analyzing his social teaching in regard to women. He did not write a social encyclical, but his significant reflection on social and moral questions is contained in numerous letters and addresses.

In an Address to women of 'Catholic-action' on 26 October 1941, Pius XII spoke of how God intended women to be mothers and created them for that purpose. The pope argued that the role of the husband was to provide subsistence for the family and that the mother's role was to 'apply vigilant diligence to caring for those thousand particulars ... which create the elements of the internal family atmosphere'.

However, the fullness of a woman's vocation is found precisely in bearing a child: 'This is the sanctity of the nuptial bed. This is the loftiness of Christian motherhood. This is the salvation of the married woman.' Pius XII dismissed women who did not want children or wanted to plan their families: 'The mother who complains because a new child presses against her bosom seeking nourishment at her breast is foolish, ignorant of herself, and unhappy.'

On 8 April 1942, Pius XII gave an Address to newlyweds on the role of husbands and wives in marriage. He argued that the honour and status of the woman were dependent on the public regard that the husband commanded, and therefore a husband 'must strive to exceed his equals and rise above them in his own field of endeavour'. Correspondingly, the woman is encouraged to be a proud and supportive wife. Any abuse of the wife is condemned, for 'the entire

8. 'Catholic-action' refers to 'all organized movements of the lay apostolate recognized as such, nationally or internationally, either by the bishops on a national level or by the Holy See'. Pius XII, *Six ans se sont*, address to the world congress of lay apostolates, 5 October 1957, sect. 3.

behaviour of the husband toward his wife must never lack natural, noble and dignified kindness and warmth'.

The following year, Pius XII outlined how women were now emerging in public life. In the Address to young women of 'Catholic-action', the pope observes that this change from 'their retired position and [now] entering nearly all the professions, hitherto fields of livelihood and action belonging exclusively to men', was as a direct consequence of the industrialization of the western world. He does not directly criticise this situation, though he does implicitly warn of its implications when he says 'ancient customs and trends, have been forced to surrender unconditionally to the modern movement'.

Toward the end of World War II, the number of women in the workforce was at an all-time high around the world. 'The modern social structure of labour, industry and the professions', observed the pope, 'demands that a large number of women, wives included, enter the fields of work and public life.' However, while this had relevance to the war-time reality, Pius XII in his 1944 Address to newly-weds did not think this situation was the social ideal. It was the law of nature and the duty and obligation of a Christian woman to establish the home, arrange for the man's well-being and to assure the family of a peaceful life together.

After the war was over, Pius XII gave an address to members of various Catholic women's associations on 21 October 1945. *Questa grande vostra adunata* (On women's duties in social and political life) was to be the most authoritative declaration of a pope on women up to that point. Pius XII was well aware of how many women had entered the workforce during the war; consequently this 1945 document, rather than promoting the high profile women had gained in western society's social and political life, argues that a woman's duties to society lie elsewhere.

He begins by affirming the dignity of women as God-given and says that the crucial question of the time is, how can that dignity be maintained and enhanced? He argues that the distinctive and complementary qualities that delineate the sexes are the ability to be married to a man and have a family or to choose voluntary celibacy in religious life.

The higher calling, in the pope's mind, is religious life. This he calls a vocation: 'This is the word which springs to our lips when we think of those girls and women who voluntarily renounce matrimony to consecrate themselves to a higher life of contemplation, sacrifice and charity.' However, there are two other choices open to women, first and most obviously motherhood, which is 'a woman's function, a woman's way, a woman's natural bent ... To this end the Creator has fashioned the whole of woman's nature: not only her organism, but also and still more her spirit and most of all her exquisite sensibility.'

The other choice Pius XII offers is the life of one who 'remains unmarried despite herself'. This call to a single life is definitely, in the pope's mind, the poorest choice and is understood, almost, in terms of personal failure: 'In the impossibility of marriage she discerns her own vocation and, sad at heart, though resigned, she too devotes herself entirely to the highest and most varied forms of beneficence.'

Returning then to the situation of the world, the pope calls on all women of all vocations outlined above to protect their dignity against 'a certain totalitarian regime [which] tempts her with marvellous promises: equality of rights with men ... assistance during gestation and labour ... public creches ... education without fees; and public assistance in the case of illness'. Pius XII conceded that there are many advantages to these social measures, but that they take away from the essential duty of a woman in society: 'Restore woman as soon as possible to her place of honour in the home as housewife and mother! This is the universal cry.'

The pope goes on to list the terrible social implications that lie ahead for society if this cry goes unheeded:

- the home of a working mother would become neglected and the family would not meet for meals or prayers;
- the children's education would suffer, especially the daughters', in their training and preparation for marriage and motherhood;
- the daughter of a working mother who 'busies herself with frivolous occupations and futile amusements, will follow her example: she will want her own freedom as soon as possible';
- the morals, religious education and personal as well as domestic pride of a working class family's daughter would be in peril;
- the working mother would age prematurely and both parents will spend their old age dependent on their children.

Therefore, every woman must do all she can to fight political doctrines and social programs that undermine the family and the home. Mothers must work inside their homes to restore them to be places which affirm their true dignity, while men deal with external affairs and public business pertaining to this same restoration.

A single woman and 'those upon whom the force of circumstances has imposed a mysterious vocation' [widowhood] are encouraged to enter into the workforce in the areas of teaching Catholic faith or 'associated ... work of man in the sphere of civil institutions, [where] she will apply herself especially to matters calling for tact, delicacy, the maternal instinct, rather than administrative rigidity'. Examples

of these works are administering orphanages, welfare work for released prisoners and rescue work for fallen girls.

As to all women's actual participation in the social and political
life of any country, Pius XII understood this only in terms of voting.
'The vote is for the Catholic woman an important means of fulfilling
her strict obligations of conscience ... her path to the voting booth
is the path of peace ... in the interests of the family and its welfare.'

Pius XII also reflected on women's roles in his teaching on moral
issues that directly affected women's lives. By 1950, abortion, con-
traception and sterilization were being promoted by some organizations and governments as necessary for birth control. In an Address
to Catholic midwives on 29 October 1951, he attacked these programs directly. In the course of his speech he placed great emphasis
on the role of mothering as a noble calling. 'And those sorrows, too,
which after original sin the mother has to suffer to bring her child
into the world, help to bind more tightly the link which unites them.
Her love is in proportion to her suffering.' The Blessed Virgin Mary
is held up as the model of an 'eager acceptance of the vocation of
motherhood! Virginal motherhood is incomparably superior to any
other, yet is a real motherhood in the true and proper meaning of the
word [vocation].' In fact, through Mary's maternity, other mothers
follow in the created order as they share in God's goodness, wisdom
and omnipotence.

This extensive survey, then, of a selection of Pius XII's teachings,
becomes an important foundation to understanding the background
of pronouncements from which Pope John Paul II writes. Woman as
virgin is the highest calling and closest to God. Woman as wife and
mother is the fulfilment of the natural order created by God. Wives
and mothers must fulfil domestic duties as their social responsibility. The single woman is a mystery, but she should devote herself to
feminine occupations. As traditional as this position might be, Pius

XII believed 'that new realities of women's lives, however doubtful their benefits might be, were here to stay and had to be confronted by the church in an informed and creative fashion.'[9]

John XXIII (1958–1963) published two social encyclicals during his four and a half year reign. Both of them had brief but important things to say to and about women.

Mater et magistra ('On Christianity and Social Progress') was published in 1961 at a time when the gap between the wealthy western nations and the developing nations was tragically clear. John called for a correction of the imbalance between rich and poor and called on all Christians to work for justice. In section 189, he turns to the issue of population and its control. In section 199, he condemns government programs and other groups who promote birth control measures and calls on women not to resort to these means as a way of halting population growth. John argues that artificial means of birth control, including sterilization, is below the human dignity of women and men.

Two years later, John XXIII published *Pacem in Terris* ('Peace on Earth'), written in response to the build-up and fear of nuclear weaponry, the erection of the Berlin Wall and the escalation of tensions between the USA and USSR. In what has become a classical approach to Catholic social teaching, John surveys the rights and responsibilities of people in the world and then looks at the signs of the times. In this context, he turns to women and sees the participation of women in the public and social life of the world as one of these signs. *Pacem in Terris* affirms women's equality to men and argues that the modern world can not tolerate women being treated as inferior or minor, in any way. Women are to be encouraged to reach their full potential for the benefit of all society.

---

9. Camp, R., 'From passive submission ...', p. 250.

Gaudium et spes ('The Pastoral Constitution of the Church in the Modern World') was approved and signed on the last working day of the Second Vatican Council, 7 December 1965. A constitution by an ecumenical council is the highest form of teaching it can issue. Because it is an articulation of an element of the faith by the bishops, under the leadership of the pope, it is teaching of the highest authority for the church.[10]

Guadium et spes was an extraordinary document for its time, as no other social teaching in the life of the church had covered such a variety of topics and issues to do with Christian life and the needs of the world. It turns its attention to the particular situation of women twice. The first occasion is in its reading of 'the signs of the times'. It notes, in section 8, that there are many imbalances in the distribution of power, wealth and opportunities in the world. 'On the family level there are tensions arising out of demographic, economic and social pressures, out of conflicts between succeeding generations, and out of new social relationships between sexes.' What the church must do is read this gender movement in the light of the gospel, and respond to it '[in] language intelligible to every generation'.

When the document looks at the duties of Christians in relation to culture, it again focuses on women in particular. It demands that all Christians work for the 'recognition and implementation everywhere of the rights of every person and civil culture in harmony with the dignity of the human person, without distinction of race, sex, nation, religion or social circumstance'.

This freedom is expressed in terms of people's rights to education, cultural expression and social development. Women become the council's example of how this must happen. 'At present women are involved in nearly all spheres of life: they ought to be permitted

---

10. See 'Teaching authority of the church', *New Catholic Encyclopedia*, New York: McGraw-Hill, vol. 13, pp. 962.

to play their part fully according to their own particular nature. It is up to everyone to see to it that women's specific and necessary participation in cultural life be acknowledged and fostered.'

The Vatican Council, then, offers us two quite different reflections on women. The first, implicitly, is in terms of wife and mother, in the image of Mary and the church, and the second is as the paradigm of human liberation in the light of the Gospel. The Council, in its closing remarks, said to women that 'the hour has come when the vocation of woman is being achieved in its fullness, the hour in which woman acquires in the world an influence, an effect and a power never hitherto achieved.' Thus it endorsed and promoted a new era of thinking about women's role and status in the church and the world.

Populorum progressio ('The Development of Peoples') was an encyclical published by Paul VI (1963–1978) on 26 March 1967. It develops the Council's thinking specifically in regard to developing nations and international responsibilities. Although Paul never directly mentions the social, religious or political role of women, he does lay down two principles of social action which pertain directly to the issue of women attaining their true dignity and discerning their vocation. The first is the principle of the right and duty of all persons to develop their qualities, and talents to the fullest degree possible. This ultimately entails developing their spiritual capacities in concert with their personal gifts. The church and society should see to it that this can happen. The second principle is that the struggle against injustice [gender injustice in this case], must be a peaceful struggle, one that works for the development of humanity as God intended it and for the good of all.

I cite *Populorum progressio* as a prelude to Paul VI's 1971 apostolic letter, *Octogesima adveniens* ('A Call to Action]') What was left unsaid about women in the 1967 encyclical is spelt out clearly in this work. Written to commemorate the eightieth anniversary of *Rerum novarum*, this letter focuses on the problem of urbanization and its consequences on women, youth, the aged, the handicapped and the socially marginalized.

Paul reaffirms women's equality with men in the sight of God, but goes further and argues that this equality gives them an equal right to participation in all facets of social, cultural, economic and political life. This is a universal truth and each local church is encouraged to read the signs of the time in its nation and to act. Later, in the same section, Paul recounts how in spite of the church's repeated call for change in the social hierarchy, discrimination on racial, gender, cultural and religious grounds still exists. Fundamental to this situation is that these structures of injustice must be eradicated and the equal participation of all people guaranteed. Members of the church must see this as a personal responsibility.

The next year, Paul VI issued an apostolic letter, *Ministeria quaedam* ('On the Question of Ministry'), reviewing minor orders[11] and establishing the procedures for the diaconate. In this revision Paul gives back to the laity the role of reading and serving but says that women are not to be admitted into the offices of lector (reader) and acolyte (server). He cites the constant tradition of the church in regard to these office as the reason why women are to be excluded.

By 1973, the western world was starting to feel the political and social pressure of the women's liberation movement. Paul VI responded to the concerns and criticisms of this movement regarding the church itself and its teachings about women in society by establishing the Commission for the Role of Women in the Church and Society. A commission has no authority of its own. It is established to study a particular issue and make recommendations to a Vatican department or to the pope. It can prepare a document which can be published only with the approval of the pope. Even when it is pub-

---

11. Such as porter, catechist, exorcist and sub-deacon.

lished it does not carry the force of teaching authority for the church but of scholarly opinion.

This commission's mandate was to discuss the role of humanity in the created order as intended by God, to look at women's roles in the church's mission of salvation, and the appropriate role of women in contemporary society in the light of *Gaudium et spes*.

On 31 January 1976, the commission presented its report to the Pope. It made recommendations to various groups: the Holy See, bishops' conferences, religious congregations, Catholic international associations and Catholic universities. To the Holy See and bishops, the commission submitted that:

— competent women should have a greater presence within the curial departments, particularly where the concerns of the issues before it affect women most directly;

— women should be given greater access to all non-ordained ministries in the liturgical and pastoral life of the church;

— all baptised Catholics be granted participation in jurisdiction in the revised code of canon law;

— women be granted more opportunities for spiritual, doctrinal and pastoral formation.

To religious congregations, the commission submitted that:

— the formation of religious takes into account the necessity of working in close collaboration with women;

— teaching orders revise the image of women and their relationship with men that they present and how they present it;

— orders work more closely with lay groups in promoting women's rights and dignity.

To Catholic lay associations the commission suggested that:

- they promote the goals and activities of the International Women's Year in their groups;
- they participate in all UN activities that work for women's betterment;
- they work more closely with religious and other church bodies to improve women's status in the church.

Finally, to Catholic universities the commission recommended that, 'In order to give the necessary theological and scientific basis to efforts aimed at improvement of man/woman relationships in the life of society and of the church, study and research should be undertaken and promoted in relevant fields – theology, philosophy, sociology, anthropology, history and at an interdisciplinary level.'

Within two years, Paul VI had approved and confirmed a document from the Sacred Congregation for the Doctrine of the Faith. The declaration on certain questions regarding the admission of women to the ministerial priesthood was published in response to requests from various bishops' conferences for a clarification of the church's stance on this issue. This is almost always the reason for such declarations from Vatican departments. They explain teaching or legislation as it pertains to new circumstances. There were at this time several demands for ordination from among Catholic women.

The argument of this declaration is that the church does not have the power to change its teaching on an exclusively male priesthood because this is an immutable truth handed down through the centuries of the church's tradition. Most of the arguments of this document hinge around this point. They are: that the Catholic church has never had a woman priest or bishop; that Jesus gave an apostolic mission only to his male apostles and not even to his mother Mary; that the early church did not have a mandate from Jesus to ordain women, so it did not do so; finally, that maleness is, therefore, an essential element of sacramental ordination.

The other argument that the congregation puts forward is that only a male can act in the person of Christ at the eucharist. 'There would not be this natural resemblance which must exist between Christ and his minister if the role of Christ were not taken by a man. In such a case it would be difficult to see in the minister the image of Christ. For Christ himself was and remains a man.'

This declaration insists that this does not take away from the dignity and vocation of women in the church. The congregation argues that, on the contrary, it adds to it, making clear the gender roles appropriate to men and women revealed by Christ in the natural order.

It is clear from this study of the documents produced during Pope Paul VI's reign that critical work was done on the contemporary status of women. Significant advances were made in articulating their rights, affirming their aspirations to public office and political status, and reflecting on their role in the church's mission up to, but certainly excluding, ordination to the priesthood. This is the immediate social tradition that John Paul II inherited.

Within six months of becoming pope, John Paul II published an encyclical, on 25 March 1978, *Redemptor hominis* ('Redeemer of Man'). In a personal statement of faith and theology, he teaches that humanity, though sinful, has been redeemed in Christ and therefore must stand firm in the face of considerable difficulties in the modern world which compromise human dignity and worth. The church's mission is to protect the rights of men and women and to promote their true vocation and destiny in Christ. While he never directly speaks of women or their particular situation, his general principles apply to them and lay the foundation for specific development at a later date.

To commemorate the ninetieth anniversary of Leo XIII's *Rerum novarum*, John Paul published a social encyclical on human work.

Laborem exercens was promulgated on 14 September 1981. 'Written almost entirely by the pope himself, the encyclical reflects statements made while he was a Polish prelate and those made during the first years of his pontificate.'[12]

Women are directly mentioned only once in this document. In the context of discussing the rights of workers to just wages and the responsibilities of workers to be just in their demands, John Paul turns to the needs of the family. He argues against women working outside the home where there is no significant economic need to do so. Rather, a 'single salary given to the head of the family for his work, sufficient for the needs of the family without the spouse having to take up gainful employment outside the home', would be the best situation. To counterbalance the economic hardships for some families this would obviously entail, the pope also argues for the just remuneration of mothers who are raising families. This, John Paul believes, demands a reappraisal of the role of mother in society and entails that society recognize the work of and the debt it owes to women in this area. The pope is strongly critical of any social or economic system that overtly or covertly insists that the mother of a family leave the home and work.

Later in the same year, the pope published an apostolic exhortation on the role of the Christian family in the world. This letter, *Familiaris consortio*, together with the later marian encyclical, *Redemptoris Mater*, form the intellectual ground from which the apostolic letter, *Mulieris dignitatem*, most immediately evolves.

Familiaris consortio comes out of the deliberations of the 1980 synod of bishops on the family. It reads the signs of the times in relation to modern-day family life and then outlines what makes a Christian family distinctive from any other family. In an extended treatment,

---

12. Heriot J., de Berrie P., Schutheis M., *Catholic Social Teaching*, New York: Orbis, p. 70.

the pope expounds the role of the each of the members of the family in the unit itself and in the church and in the world. Finally, the exhortation argues that the family should be looked after with greater tenacity and care.

For our purposes, three sections of this long document are relevant. In section 16, John Paul finishes off his discussion on the distinctive characteristics of a Christian family by speaking about the complementarity between a life of virginity and celibacy and marriage. He does this by observing how the respect given to marriage by a society is usually in measure to the respect given to celibacy. 'When marriage is not esteemed neither can consecrated virginity or celibacy exist.'

The Pope also states that virginity and celibacy in the church protects the 'mystery of marriage and defends it from any reduction and impoverishment'. This occurs because the virgin anticipates the heavenly marriage of Christ to the church and bears witness to it in this world.

For this reason, the church has always 'defended the superiority of this charism to that of marriage, by reason of the wholly singular link which it has with the kingdom of God'. Because of this charism, the consecrated religious goes on to be father and mother of many and cooperates with families in witnessing to the virtues of 'fidelity, sacrifice, mortification and self denial'.

In the discussion on the roles of individual members of the family, the pope draws quite direct attention to the situation of women. This is in response to the attention that they received in the debates of the synod on the family.

John Paul makes three points in relation to Christian anthropology and women's status:

  — women have equal dignity with men and consequently they have 'inalienable rights proper to a human person';

— 'God manifests the dignity of women in the highest form possible by assuming human flesh from the Virgin Mary … and presenting her as the model of redeemed woman';

— the works and actions of Jesus towards women confirm their dignity and equality in the sight of God. This can be observed especially in the Easter appearance of Jesus to a woman before the other disciples.

Familiaris consortio goes on to recognize that the modern world is transforming the idea that women are exclusively meant to be wives and mothers. It warns against this move, when a fruitful family life is the price that has to be paid: '… true advancement of women requires that clear recognition be given to the value of their maternal and family role, by comparison with all other public roles and other professions.' The pope goes on to recapitulate his points made in *Laborem exercens* that women must 'not in practice be compelled to work outside the home'.

What all this requires of men, the document concludes, is that men 'truly esteem and love women'. The pope warns against women renouncing their femininity to imitate men inside or outside the home.

Finally, John Paul calls for an end to any offence against the dignity of women where they are regarded 'not as a person but as a thing, an object of trade, or the service of selfish interest and mere pleasure'. To this end he calls the whole church to action so that 'the image of God that shines in all human beings without exception may be fully respected'.

Chaper 2

Women in Mariologolical Teaching

A COMMON MISCONCEPTION about papal teaching is that Mary has been the focus of an inordinate amount of attention. In authoritative official documents, at least, this is not true. In comparison with the body of social teaching we have just looked at, teaching about Mary is very small indeed. But it is critical in terms of the discussion of women's role and dignity.

Leo XIII's encyclical on the rosary, *Magnae Dei matris*, published 8 September 1892, is one of several documents on devotion to Mary through the rosary. Leo draws attention to the great role model Mary is for all believers: 'If we, with her powerful help, should dedicate ourselves wholly and entirely to this undertaking [imitation of Mary], we can portray at least an outline of such great virtue and sanctity.' Women who are mothers are encouraged above all others to follow her example. 'Mary well knows what is [our nature's] condition and is the best and most solicitous of mothers.'

In 1904 Pius X published his one and only encyclical on Mary, *Ad diem illum* ('On the Immaculate Conception'). In it, Pius celebrates the 50th anniversary of the proclamation of the Dogma of the Immaculate Conception. He expounds the theme of the imitation of Mary in section 16: 'Whoever, then, wishes – and no one ought not so to wish – that their devotion should be perfect and worthy of her, should go further and strive to the utmost to imitate her example.'

He concludes this section by calling attention to Mary's example in virginity. Citing St Ambrose, he writes, 'Such was Mary ... that her life is an example for all ... Have then before your eyes, as an image, the virginity and life of Mary from whom as from a mirror shines forth the brightness of chastity and the form of virtue.'

On Christmas day 1931, Pius XI issued an encyclical entitled *Lux veritatis* ('Light of Truth'). A document celebrating the 15th centenary of the Council of Ephesus, it begins as the Council did, expounding the person and work of Jesus, and concludes with a celebration of the 'divine motherhood of the Blessed Virgin Mary'. In this setting, Pius addresses himself to how mothers, especially 'those mothers of our day who, wearied of childbearing or of the matrimonial bond, have neglected or violated the obligation they assumed, should look and meditate intently upon Mary.' In doing so he hopes that these mothers will receive, through the Queen of Heaven, the grace to 'become ashamed of the dishonour branded on the great sacrament of matrimony and be moved, as far as possible, to attain to her wonderfully exalted virtues'.

Mariology during the years 1939–1958 reached great heights. In 1942 the world was consecrated to the Immaculate Heart of Mary. In 1943, Mary was the focal point of Pope Pius XII's epilogue to his encyclical, *Mystici corporis* ('On the Mystical Body of Christ'). The year 1945 was declared to be a Marian Year, with the new feast of the 'Queenship of Mary' being instituted. Norms were laid down in the pope's 1947 encyclical, *Mediator Dei* ('On the Sacred Liturgy'), regarding approved forms of Marian devotion. Of greatest significance was the defining of the Dogma of the Assumption of Blessed Virgin Mary in 1950. What is striking about all this marian teaching is the broad way Pius XII interprets Mary as model. She is not a paradigm only or especially for women, but is consistently held up as a model for all. *Fulgens corona gloriae* ('On the Marian Year'), the encyclical letter of 1953, states that 'Christians should conform their lives to the example of the Virgin ... [for she] ... urges us to that innocence and integrity of life which flees from and abhors even the slightest stain of sin.'

The following year, Pius XII wrote *Sacra virginitas* ('On Holy Virginity'), an encyclical letter on religious life, which was, in the western world, experiencing tremendous growth in numbers and works at the time. Religious life was also the focus of criticism and condemnation by people outside the church who saw its lifestyle, particularly its chastity, as unnatural and abnormal. Pius XII replied to these objections and extolled the virtues of consecrated virginity. Right at the end of his reflection he spoke directly to those in religious life, both women and men. The repeated experience of the church had been, Pius argued, that 'perfect and unsullied chastity' had been accompanied by 'a solid and very lively devotion to the Virgin Mother of God ... the mistress of virginity'. Women, though, have special claim on Mary in this regard, says the pope, quoting St Ambrose, 'She is the one you imitate, daughters ... She is the image of virginity. For such was Mary that her life by itself alone is teaching enough for all.'

The Second Vatican Council did not publish a document on Mary. Instead, it looks at the role of Mary in *Lumen gentium* ('The Dogmatic Constitution on the Church'), approved and signed on 21 November 1964. This document never speaks directly to women, or about women. However, in chapter 8, on 'Our Lady', the bishops expound the function of Mary in the history of salvation, the relationship between Mary and the church, appropriate devotion to Mary, and Mary as a sign of hope for all humanity. Within this section, it is paragraph 63 that Pope John Paul II refers to, repeatedly, as a support for his teaching that a woman's vocation is as a virgin and mother. 'For in the mystery of the church, which is itself rightly called virgin and mother, the Blessed Virgin stands out in eminent and singular fashion as exemplar both of virgin and mother.'

Marialis cultus ('On Devotion to Mary') was Paul VI's major contribution to mariology. It was published as an apostolic exhortation on 2 February 1974, with the explicit intention of updating Marian devotional practices in line with the spirit of the age and the teaching of the Council. Pope Paul is at pains to place Mary in a christological frame of reference. Consequently, unlike his predecessors in several of the documents we have looked at above, Jesus, not Mary, is held up as the primary person to imitate. 'Christ is the only way to the Father, and ultimate example to whom the disciple must conform [his] own conduct.'

Mary remains a model of holiness, a reason for divine hope, an intercessor and a powerful aid for all men and women who strive to become like Jesus, 'within whose mystery … [man] alone finds true light'. This movement away from presenting Mary as the model for all believers and as the prototype for virgins and mothers is an extremely important development of the Catholic tradition's reflection on the role of Mary in people's lives.

We noted earlier on page 29 that *Familiaris consortio* lays the foundation for *Mulieris dignitatem's* reflection on the social situation of women in the family and society. In the same way it can be seen that *Redemptoris Mater* provides the context in which *Mulieris dignitatem* explores the relationship between Mary and women.

Redemptoris Mater ('The Mother of the Redeemer') heralded the beginning of the Marian Year which the pope designated to begin on 7 June 1987. A long and detailed letter, it looks at Mary in relation to Christ, then in relation to the church, and finally as a reflection of true and full maternity.

It is in this final section that the pope takes up Mary's relationship with women directly. While Mary is a model and image for all people, she 'takes on special importance in relation to women and their status'. The pope teaches that this is true in four ways:

- Mary, through being the mother of Jesus, foreshadows God's great blessings on womanhood generally;
- through Mary's free co-operation in the incarnation, all women can 'find in her the secret of living their femininity with dignity and of achieving their own true advancement';
- the church, consequently, celebrates the greatest virtues of women in celebrating Mary;
- Mary remains a model for women in 'the self-offering totality of love; the strength that is capable of bearing the greatest sorrows; limitless fidelity and tireless devotion to work; the ability to combine penetrating intuition with words of support and encouragement"

This view of Mary is the one that the pope wanted to promote during the Marian Year, for it expressed most clearly 'the special bond between humanity and this mother'. It is important to note that just as this encyclical proclaimed the Marian Year open so did *Mulieris dignitatem* close it.

Conclusion

From this survey of papal statements on women from 1891 to 1987, the distinctive contribution of what John Paul II was going to do in 1988 becomes clear. In reflecting on women's role in the church and society, Pope John Paul brings together the social doctrine and mariological traditions into one document. Up to this time, previous popes had chosen to keep these areas, and the scope of their respective interests, separate. John Paul II sees no need to do this and inaugurates a new era in approaching the questions about women that confront the church today. The implication of his approach is that he holds that one area illuminates the other and so the fusion of the two traditions only clarifies and develops the church's reflection on the matter.

John Paul II maintains that in Mary's earthly life and through her role in salvation she discloses for all people the essential Christian truth about women's role in the Christian community and the wider society. In arguing this, John Paul calls upon the entire tradition he has inherited from his predecessors this century and develops what he describes as the 'truth about the human being, man and woman', a truth that is revealed in Christ and in the 'woman who was the mother of Christ. This is precisely what is meant to be the common thread running throughout the present document [*Mulieris dignitatem*] which fits into the broader context of the Marian Year.'

Part Two

Women in
Mulieris dignitatem
and Ordinatio sacerdotalis

Chapter 3

The Teaching of Pope John Paul II on Women

THE SIGNIFICANCE of *Mulieris dignitatem* in the study of papal teaching on women cannot be exaggerated. It is the longest and most complex document ever written by any pope at any time on the dignity and vocation of women. It summarizes many of the positions previous popes have articulated, and departs from them in significant ways.

Mulieris dignitatem is quoted in relation to women in *The Catechism of the Catholic Church* and, together with the *Declaration on the question of ordaining women to the ministerial priesthood*, they are the cornerstones on which *Ordinatio sacerdotalis* is built. For many years to come these documents will be the most important literature from the Catholic Church's magisterium on the subject of women. They demand special attention and study.

The status and authority of *Mulieris dignitatem*

Mulieris dignitatem is an apostolic letter. It is published as a twofold guide to the people of the church on the issue of women's vocation and dignity. First, it restates the church's position on the anthropological and theological concepts involved in this issue as they pertain to the church's pastoral life. Second, it directs men and women in the conduct of their lives as a consequence of this theology. It is not an infallible document. The position taken in it is in no way definitive but is the wisdom of the teaching church at that present time in relation to present circumstances. Therefore, it is a pastoral exposition that enables Catholics to clarify their own theological reflections and personal actions against the stated position of the teaching church. While it does present a definite opinion on several points that have been under discussion in the church for some time, it does not close the debate on any of them, except one

This point is the question of women's ordination to the priesthood. Here *Mulieris dignitatem* states that, given the reasons it has just outlined, that the eucharist is a paradigm of Ephesians 5 and that men are 'a clear and unambiguous' sign of the '*persona Christi*': 'this explanation confirms the teaching of the Declaration [of the Congregation for the Doctrine of the Faith], *Inter insigniores*.' This declaration stated that the church had no authority from Christ to ordain women. Consequently, *Mulieris dignitatem*, in confirming this position, redefines the official church's position on this issue explicitly.

Apart from this exception then, this apostolic letter demands what has been termed 'true internal assent'.[13] In other words, the 'venerable brothers and dear sons and daughters' to whom the letter is addressed are expected to listen respectfully to its argument as they would listen to the argument of any person qualified within a particular discipline, someone who is competent to teach. On the basis of this listening, each person makes his or her own judgement about the dignity and vocation of women in the church and the world.

Mulieris dignitatem is a response to a number of forces. It is part of the wide-ranging discussion that has taken place on the role and status of women over recent years in the secular world. It continues

---

13. See Lerch, J. R., 'Teaching authority of the church', *The Catholic Encyclopedia*, vol. 13, 1970, p. 965.

the church's teaching on women's dignity which has had prominence since the pontificate of Pius XII. And it flows directly out of the October 1987 synod of bishops, which considered the 'vocation and mission of the laity in the church and in the world, tewnty years after the Second Vatican Council'.

One of the conclusions of this synod, which the pope makes his own and declares to be the purpose of this work, is that 'a further study of the anthropological and theological bases ... is needed in order to solve the problems connected with the meaning and dignity of being a woman and being a man.'

It is not without significance that this teaching is issued at the close of a year John Paul II designated as a 'Marian Year'. The document explores the relationship between 'the Mother of Christ' and the women of the church.

Mary, women and their essential dignity

Mulieris dignitatem begins by situating Mary as the 'woman-mother of God [*Theotokos*]'. The woman of Genesis 3 is equated with the woman of Galatians 4:4. 'Therefore, a woman is present in the central salvific event which marks the fullness of time: this event is realized in her and through her.' Hence, Mary is invited into the ultimate and unutterable mysterious relationship which engulfs her being and attains 'a union with God that exceeds all the expectations of the human spirit'.

Through this union with Mary:

— God foreshadows God's invitation to us all by inviting her into close union with Jesus. In this, she is our representative.

— God calls Mary to the union of motherhood, which only

woman can fulfil. Hence Mary is venerated in the church as *Theotokos*, Mother of God.

However, Mary's role as Mother of God is not just one of glory and honour. Mary's decision, made with full volition, to enter into God's plan for salvation also, at one and the same time, made her God's servant. Mary as the handmaid of the Lord becomes the paradigm for all people who serve God in Christ. 'Mary takes her place within Christ's service', and reveals for both men and women the degree to which union with God calls for a full and unremitting response of self. Mary's example is a model for all women.

Mulieris dignitatem begins this discussion by focusing on the book of Genesis. From the beginning of God's revelation in scripture, 'both man and woman are human beings to an equal degree, both are created in God's image.' Consequently, the creation of woman, from man's rib (in Genesis 2:18-25), to be his helpmate, is not a statement of subordination of woman to man but, in the light of their intrinsic equality, is another way of affirming their essential origin and identity.

This equality in God's image is demonstrated in our ability to be 'rational and free creatures capable of knowing God and loving [him]'. Added to these supreme gifts is humanity's need for a mutual relationship where men and women need each other. This is a reflection of the divine communion, 'a prelude to the definitive self-revelation of the Triune God'. These are the principles of anthropology *Mulieris dignitatem* understands to be the indispensable point of departure for Christianity. '[Man] is created in the image and likeness of God ... to exist for others, to become a gift.'

As well as this anthropological truth, the scriptures also reveal the theological basis of what God is like. The Hebrew scriptures demonstrate the masculine and feminine attributes of God not in any sense of capturing God definitively but in trying to express God's incomprehensibility. The limits of our language about God are significant and our human-centred (anthropomorphic) analogies reveal both God's identification with the best traits of God's creatures (fidelity and motherhood) and also God's otherness. The Christian scriptures also illustrate this point. The *Abba* of Jesus is not fatherly in a human way, but in an 'ultra-corporeal, superhuman and completely divine sense'. Thus, in describing God as father or mother, the scriptures affirm what we can, and can not, say about the reality of God.

Having established the basic tenets of the anthropological and theological approaches in this study, the document applies them to studying how the equality between women and men became distorted. God's original desire that men and women be equal was frustrated. The manifestation of this un-likeness in Genesis 2:18-25 shows that sin has not destroyed our likeness to God but our identity has been obscured and our relationship with each other has been diminished in our ability to reflect God's face in the world.

A consequence of human sinfulness is clearly seen in Genesis 3:16 in which the author declares: 'Your desire shall be for your husband, and he shall also rule over you.' Thereby patriarchy, the structural domination of men over women, is an initial manifestation of humanity's ruptured relationship with God – original sin. 'This domination indicates the disturbance and loss of the stability of that fundamental equality which the man and woman possess.'

However, God has remained faithful to creation through redeeming everything about it, including this domination of male over female. For just as Eve was mother of the fall, so Mary is mother of the restoration. Mary, the New Eve, 'is the new beginning of the dignity and vocation of each and every woman'. Mary's life becomes a model for all women because her role in redemption came through the 'discovery of her own feminine humanity'. She is the fulfilment of Eve, the archetype of Christian womanhood, and the mother of human salvation. God at work in Mary declares the special mission and status of all women.

Jesus' relationship
to women

Having established Mary as the mother of redemption, *Mulieris dignitatem* then focuses on Jesus, the cause of salvation, and argues that his life reveals the honour owed to all women. Taking John's account of Jesus and the Samaritan woman (John 4:1-42) as striking evidence that Jesus defended women's dignity against the mores of first century Palestine, it argues that he directly opposed the tradition of male domination and disregard for women that were an accepted part of his day. In fact, respect for and solidarity with women is a sign of the kingdom Jesus proclaimed.

As a result of this new ethos, many women were attracted to the kingdom Jesus proclaimed. This is obvious when one considers how many women are spoken of in the New Testament. Because of the encounter women had with Jesus, several of them travelled with him and financed his ministry. Women also appear in the parables of Jesus and some, like the poor widow who gave all she had (Luke 21:1-4), emerge from the story 'as a model for everyone ... for in the socio-judicial system of the time widows were totally defenceless people'. Jesus does not take the part of women just because he sees them as socially outcast, but because 'he knows the dignity of man, his worth in God's eyes'. Jesus' ministry to women is a result of his union with God's original vision of equal personhood.

An example of how Jesus entered 'into the concrete and historical situation which is weighed down by the inheritance of sin' is illustrated in John 8:3-11. The woman is caught in the act of adultery.

However, Jesus can see her conscience, her state of sinfulness, and takes her part; in doing so he confronts the injustice and sinfulness of her male attackers. Consequently, we see in this story the extent to which Jesus worked for the dignity of women in his day. However this companionship is not just for that era. It is for everyone in every age. All women who love Christ feel liberated by this truth that they have equal dignity. Restored to themselves, they feel loved with eternal love. Christ calls all women to share in the attributes of a disciple: to listen, to be taught and to profess profound faith (John 4;14; 11:15; 11:21-27). The fidelity of the women to Jesus in his passion and death (John 19:25; Matthew 27:55; Luke 23:27) is the model of all women in their response to Christ. Jesus had an appreciation and admiration for this distinctively feminine response.

The clearest example of this feminine response, *Mulieris dignitatem* argues, is in women's sensitivity to Christ. In the resurrection, Mary Magdalene embodies this virtue. Mary Magdalene is the first witness to the empty tomb. She is the 'apostle to the Apostles' and being so, witnesses to the faith, respect and trust that Jesus has for all women. What was true of Mary Magdalene is true for all now, as the Spirit at Pentecost is poured out equally on all and leads the daughters to prophesy (Joel 3:1). Each woman is called 'to express by one's words and one's life the mighty works of God (Acts 2:11)'.

A woman's vocation to virginity or motherhood

Having established the mandate women have from Jesus to respond to the work of the kingdom, *Mulieris dignitatem* now defines the practical implication of this response by returning to the life and example of Mary the mother of Jesus.

A woman has a two-dimensional vocation: virginity and motherhood. This is exemplified perfectly in Mary. 'Virginity and motherhood co-exist in her … Indeed, the person of the Mother of God helps everyone, especially women, to see how these two dimensions, these two paths in the vocation of women as persons, explain and complete each other.'

The vocation of motherhood is seen to have dual significance. First, motherhood, placed within the context of the conjugal relationship, is seen as a great giving of self. Although both parents are charged with responsibility for care of the children, it is the mother who has the more demanding and crucial role. The document outlines how, theologically, motherhood participates in the generating life of the Trinity, and as a result has a special place in the sight of God. This role should be recognized by the world as a special debt owed to women for being mothers. Because of the physiological process involved in carrying and bearing a child, 'women are more capable then men of paying attention to another person, and motherhood develops this predisposition even more.'

Second, the self-giving of motherhood is akin to the process of salvation history. Motherhood, like the covenant, is a sign of God's action in the world and makes manifest God's own self-giving. This is especially clear in the incarnation, through Mary's maternal role. Consequently, 'each and every time that motherhood is repeated in human history, it is always related to the covenant which God established with the human race through the motherhood of the Mother of God.'

The other vocation of women, until marriage or for life, is virginity. In the teaching of Christ, motherhood is connected with virginity, but also distinct from it. Some women, in responding to Christ through their feminine nature, choose celibacy. Celibacy is both a gift from God and choice made in full freedom. 'Celibacy for the sake of the kingdom' (Matthew 19:12) was an innovation of Jesus, the document argues. In taking up this option, a woman in consecrated virginity follows Jesus and the radical example he lived. However, virginity is also spousal in character. In the 'vocation to virginity [women] find Christ first of all ... and they respond to this gift with a sincere gift of their whole lives ... They thus give themselves to the divine Spouse.'

A life consecrated to virginity means excluding the possibility of marriage and, therefore, physical motherhood. However, the relationship between the two vocations is profound when one takes into account the nature of spiritual motherhood in the life led by women who are celibate for the kingdom. In this vocation, a consecrated woman finds Christ, her Spouse, in the people to whom she ministers. Just as a mother in response to Christ is ready to be of service to her children, so too a religious woman demonstrates her love for Christ in apostolic service. This is the point of convergence between the two dimensions of a woman's vocation. This convergence centres on the free act of self-giving of the bride to the groom.

By way of summary, then, *Mulieris dignitatem* reiterates that anyone who considers the practicalities of a woman's vocation in the light of the gospel must take into account three points. First, 'the superiority of virginity over marriage which is a constant teaching of the church' (1 Corinthians 7:38; Matthew 19:10-12). This does not diminish the importance of motherhood but emphasizes the radical nature of celibacy. Second, the identification of the church as a mother and virgin, analogous to Mary's maternity and virginity: for, while the church 'keeps whole and pure the fidelity she has pledged to the Spouse', the church 'by her preaching and by baptism ... brings forth to a new and immortal life children who are conceived by the Holy Spirit and born of God'. Third, unless people understand the dialectic of the relationship of mother and virgin through Mary, the mother of God, through the church and through the vocation of woman, they will have an inadequate 'hermeneutic of man, or of what is human'. However, to understand this relationship is to 'appreciate and appropriate what is feminine ... in the perspective of our faith, the mystery of woman ... virgin-mother-spouse'.

The church as bride

Mulieris dignitatem takes the practical teaching it has just outlined with regard to a woman's vocation and applies it to the church. Ephesians 5:25-33 teaches that the church is the bride of Christ. This relationship is spousal in character and is a model for the church in its reflections on woman's spousal relationship to Christ and to man. God in Christ is the spouse, the bridegroom of the church, and this analogy expresses God's relationship with humanity. However, 'reading this rich and complex passage, which, taken as a whole is a great analogy, we must distinguish that element which expresses the human reality of interpersonal relations from that which expresses in symbolic language the great mystery which is divine.'

These important distinctions, the document argues, are to be understood in three ways:

— Ephesians 5:25-33 is not reinforcing the domination
of women by men. The subjugation St Paul calls for in
this passage is based on respect and equality. 'It is to be
understood and carried out in a new way: as a mutual
subjection out of reverence for Christ.'
— While this mutual respect and obedience is true for
marriage, it is not true for the church where 'the
subjection is only on the part of the church' to Christ.
Married people must live out their subjugation in terms of
equal authority and dignity under the headship of Christ.
The truth of equal and mutual obedience of women
to men, men to women, and all to Christ, as revealed

here, is 'the ethos of the Redemption [which] is clear and definitive'.

— Ephesians 5 provides a symbolic ecclesiology. The analogy of Christ the bridegroom taking his bride, the church, to himself is just that — an analogy. Therefore it 'implies a likeness, while at the same time leaving ample room for non-likeness'.

As a result of these distinctions, the analogy can speak of the church as a bride, even when men constitute over half the church, because here the analogy has a non-likeness to the married relationship. What it expresses is not so much a metaphor of spousal literalism, but a concept of how Christ, the redeemer of all that is masculine and feminine in humanity, is present to the church. The Christian community is the place where 'masculinity and femininity are distinct yet, at the same time, complete and explain each other'. Christ's love as the symbolically male bridegroom becomes the 'model and pattern of all human love, men's love in particular'.

The document then goes on to elucidate how, in the context of this ecclesiology of the spousal relationship between Christ and the church, the call of the twelve and their sacramental ministry can be properly understood. Jesus, acting 'in a completely free and sovereign manner, chose only men to be apostles. Jesus could have chosen women, if he wanted to, but did not do so. To these twelve men at the Last Supper, and on Easter Sunday, a sacramental mission was given in terms of the eucharist and reconciliation (Luke 22:19; 1 Corinthians 11:24; John 20:23). This mission, through its relationship to Christ, expresses the spousal love of the Bridegroom for the church. Consequently, on two levels men legitimate the divine order in sacramental ministry: firstly, their maleness establishes a clear and unambiguous link with the *persona Christi*; second, it 'expresses the relationship between what is feminine and what is masculine ... [as] willed by God both in the mystery of creation and in the mystery of Redemption.' As a result, women cannot be admitted to the ministerial priesthood.

So, although women are excluded from the ordained ministry in the Catholic Church, all women and men are called to respond as fully as they can to Christ the bridegroom with self-giving service. This is the priesthood of all believers, the gift of Christ's bride. At the forefront of this ministry is the pursuit of holiness. Christ's church as a hierarchy of holiness has, as its model and pinnacle, Mary of Nazareth. 'In this sense, one can say that the church is both Marian and Apostolic-Petrine.' Also present in this communion of holiness are the great women of the church's history. These 'holy woman are incarnations of the feminine ideal; they are also a model for all Christians, a model of the *sequela Christi* [follower of Christ], and example of how the Bride must respond with love to the love of the Bridegroom.'

In conclusion, then, *Mulieris dignitatem* restates why it is necessary, and of moment, that a document such as this should be written. Given the many calls for changes in the dignity and vocation of women, even in the life of the church, human development must be in harmony with the teaching of Christ. The truth of Christ's words and actions are immutable. While developments in women's situation in our time can be good, a path that is different to Christ's path would lead to doubtful if not erroneous and deceptive results.

A woman's mission to love

It is precisely in the order of love, the document argues, that the real value and dignity of women is discovered. From the Genesis account to the Ephesians analogy, to its fullest expression in Mary the mother of God, 'woman is the one in whom the order of love in the created world of persons takes first root'. And while this call to love pertains to all humanity, it has a special manifestation in woman because of her femininity. This feminine love has no cultural or individual boundaries and is independent of social constraints and, in union with Mary the mother of God, it reaches its 'fullest and most direct [expression] – the intimate linking of the order of love … with the Holy Sprit'.

The true vocation of women, then, is this same love which defines their dignity and also defines their mission. 'Woman can only find herself by giving love to others.' This feminine loving, this womanly mission, is one of being entrusted with people's lives, as a natural or spiritual mother. This is the genius which belongs to women, and which can ensure sensitivity for human beings in every circumstance because they are human and because the greatest of all the gifts of humanity is love (1 Corinthians 13:13).

Finally, the document reminds readers how in Jesus' conversation with the woman at the well (in John 4:1-42) Jesus challenged the woman to recognize the 'gift of God' for the 'sincere gift of self'. So too the church must thank God, particularly during the Marian Year, for all the manifestations of the feminine 'genius' and 'all the fruits of feminine holiness'.

Ordinatio sacerdotalis

The people calling for the ordination of women were not deterred by the declaration of the Congregation in 1977 or *Mulieris dignitatem* in 1988. Many scholars continued to research and publish on the questions surrounding the ordination of women.

It was also rumoured that bishops in several countries, contending with a shortage of male celibate priests and seeing the pastoral competence of many women in parishes and chaplaincy, were beginning to believe that the time for the ordination of women was near.

The Anglican Communion had begun to ordain women and this had led to some Church of England clergymen seeking admittance into the priesthood of the Roman Catholic Church. Several Catholics, in the secular media, stated that the acceptance of these priests was a mistake, as the Church of Rome would soon be ordaining women itself.

Meanwhile the Orthodox churches resolutely stood by their tradition of male clergy and declared that it would be impossible for them to unite with a church that ordains women.

In this context, on 22 May 1994, John Paul II issued an apostolic letter, *Ordinatio sacerdotalis* ('On Priestly Ordination'). Addressed to his 'venerable brothers in the episcopate', it was issued 'in order that all doubt may be removed regarding a matter of great importance, a matter which pertains to the church's divine constitution itself, in virtue of my ministry of confirming the brethren [see Luke 22:32] I declare that the church has no authority whatsoever to confer priestly ordination on women and that this judgement is to be definitively held by all the church's faithful.'

The letter itself is very brief and begins by recalling Paul VI's response to the then Archbishop of Canterbury, Donald Coggan. Paul tells Dr Coggan that because Christ chose men to be his apostles, and that has been the constant practice of the church, women are excluded from the priesthood, 'in accordance with God's plan for his church'.

John Paul goes on to state again that the church is not authorized to admit women to the priesthood because it can only follow Christ's example. Christ, the pope argues, 'acted in a completely free and sovereign manner' which in turn the Apostles handed on to the church.

The pope then turns to Mary, as he does in *Mulieris dignitatem*, to argue that this teaching in no way discriminates against women.

'The fact that the Blessed Virgin Mary ... received neither the mission proper to the Apostles nor the ministerial priesthood clearly shows that the non-admission to priestly ordination cannot mean that women are of lesser dignity.' Consequently, generations of women in the church have 'given service to God and of the Gospel' by being martyrs, virgins and mothers.

Finally, John Paul dismisses the argument that this teaching is 'merely disciplinary', and therefore open to change, by stating that it is part of the constitution of the church.

The final paragraph of the letter carries with it all the authority a pope can use in his teaching or legislative roles, short of declaring the teaching infallible. Jesuit canon lawyer and theologian Francis Sullivan has argued that we have never seen a document like it before.[14] The wording of the final paragraph is couched in such a way as to draw on the authority of infallibility without defining it as such. This paragraph, and its implications, will be the source of intense study for years to come.

---

14. Sullivan F., 'New claims for the pope', *The Tablet*, 19 June 1994, pp.767 ff.

Part Three

*What have woman
gained and lost
in this teaching?*

Chapter 4

Reactions to the Teaching

BECAUSE *Mulieris dignitatem* generally summarizes the positions of earlier papal thought, it is a helpful place to begin to explore the impact of this teaching on women. It will become clear, however, at what points John Paul II departs from this earlier teaching. This first section, then, is based on most of the commentaries that have been written on *Mulieris dignitatem*, and gathers together into a coherent order the diversity of criticisms commentators have made of this document.

Second, we will also discuss the points where *Mulieris dignitatem* intersects with the concerns of Christian feminists. This is done to demonstrate that these respective parties are not totally opposed to one another, but agree on many critical issues in regard to women's dignity and rights.

Put simply, wherever *Mulieris dignitatem* speaks of women's status in the world – namely, women as equal to men; patriarchy (in the social sense) as sin; condemnation of any abuse of women; co-equal responsibility for the family – most writers and theologians applaud the document for its insight and reasoned argument. What is true for this document equally applies to papal statements over the last century. Placed in historical context, the pope's concerns about women, on a social level, were generally well received.

However, many writers take issue with the document when it turns to women's role in the life of the church. This is focused in the analogy which the document draws between Mary's life and mission and that of contemporary women. Most commentators believe the mariology presented, and its assumptions regarding gender roles, motherhood and virginity and priesthood, do not accord women ecclesiastically the same equality and opportunity which it argues for them socially. This type of public criticism of papal teaching on women, which has its roots in the late 1960s, has no parallel to anything in the previous seventy years.

Women's status: equal to men

The first major development in *Mulieris dignitatem* is the direct and clear affirmation that women are equal in dignity and status to men. This does not occur because of some special concession that is now afforded to women as a result of other social aspirations; their equality is ontological, an absolute principle of Christian anthropology. Women deserve the same respect as men because both share in the image of God.

Critics have welcomed this emphasis on the basic dignity of women. A typical judgement is that of theologian Mary Ann Glendon who notes that in contrast to the secular emphasis on women's rights, Pope John Paul focuses on women's dignity. 'In my view, this is a good sign ... It alerts us to the irony in our contemporary situation where women have more rights than ever before, yet their dignity, their intrinsic worth as human beings, is jeopardized in a variety of ways that seem to be distinctively modern.'[15]

Some scholars have applauded this papal reflection because its cornerstone is clearly the equal participation of men and women in God.[16] Others have argued that this foundation establishes the

---

15. Glendon, M. A., 'A greater attention to women's dignity', *L'Osservatatore Romano*, 45 (1988), p. 5.

16. Baum, G., 'Bulletin: The apostolic letter *Mulieris dignitatem*', *Concilium*, 106, (199), pp. 145f; Coste, R., 'La lettre apostolique *Mulieris dignitatem* de Jean Paul II sur la dignité et la vocation de la femme', *Esprit et Vie*, 45 (1988), pp. 611-612.

criteria that will guide the next generation in making choices that affect women, the context in which events in regard to women will be interpreted, and the basis from which sexist structures that discriminate against women will be criticized.[17]

Patriarchy as sin

Mulieris dignitatem inaugurates a new era in official church teaching in its treatment of the consequences of original sin. It affirms, on the one hand, the equality men and women share as a result of their being God's creation, and confronts the issue of what went wrong in this gender harmony. A correlation is made between the rupture of the relationship between God and humanity and the oppression of women by men.

While the document does not directly name this situation patriarchal, it does talk of 'domination' as the manifestation of the 'disturbance of that original relationship between man and woman, which corresponds to their individual dignity as persons'. As it takes Genesis 3:16 as the source text in regard to this issue, it would have been inappropriate for it to name this domination as patriarchal. This biblical text does not reflect patriarchy as such. But just as this domination was a consequence of 'original sin' so too is patriarchy a consequence of this domination. The difference is that the distortion of the relationship as described in the Genesis account concerns only a single couple, whereas patriarchy is an institutionalized process of presuming men's rights and dignities over women's rights and dignities.

This part of the letter does address many feminists' concerns, namely, that 'patriarchy as a social system based on the absolute and

17. Summerton, D., 'Pope John Paul II on women', *Vidyajyoti Journal of Theological Reflection*, 53, (1987), p. 219; Vauzan, P.,'*Mulieris dignitatem*: reazioni, contenuti e prospettive', *La Civilta Cattolica*, 139 (November 1988), pp. 250f.

unaccountable power over wives, children, slaves, servants ... and real property enjoyed by the pater-familias, that is, the father who is head of the family, tribe or clan', is sinful.[18]

Canadian theologian Gregory Baum notes that what this document establishes is the context for further questions to be asked. For example, given that domination of women by men is sinful, what is the path to repentance and conversion? What symbols would best express the re-union of men and women celebrating their unity and equality? How will we see the redemption of women from this sin taking concrete shape in the life of the church today?[19]

Condemnation of the abuse of women

The pope, in this letter, directly confronts the secular world's disordered objectification of women. He condemns the abuse of women and anything that dehumanizes them, particularly sexual objectification. He points out that contemporary applications of this fixation can be seen in abortion, the desertion by the man of a pregnant woman, and in all the many ways that women are abused by men in society. In strong language, he deplores anything that takes away from equal respect and dignity for women. In so doing the pope is not saying anything new. He is in continuity with the church's social teaching since the Vatican Council on this issue. However, *Mulieris dignitatem's* particular contribution to this teaching lies in telling men that they not only offend the rights of women in abusing them, but also deprive themselves of their own God-bestowed self-worth.

This aspect of the document has been well received by all commentators, for it affirms the truth of what contemporary feminists in

---

18. Schneiders, S., *Woman and the World*, Mahwah, New Jersey: Paulist Press, 1986, p. 11.
19. Baum, G., 'Bulletin ...', p. 145.

the church and in the secular world have been saying for years: that violence toward women has been institutionalized. Consequently, as ethicist Lisa Sowle Cahill argues, this socially acceptable abuse of women's sexuality has frequently legitimated 'physical violence, including rape, genital mutilation, coercive sterilization, abortion and murder'.[20]

Co-equal responsibility for the family

We have already noted, earlier, how Pope John Paul's encyclical letter of 1986, *Familiaris consortio*, was in many ways a precursor to *Mulieris dignitatem*. *Familiaris consortio* addressed itself to women's issues through looking at the situation of family life. It pointed out to the church and to the world that if the family is subjected to more pressure and given no assistance then its demise will be the cause of a major social crisis.

The influence of this encyclical on *Mulieris dignitatem* is evident in the issue of parents' joint obligations toward their children. Commentators have noted that while the situation of the family has remained constant, what has changed between 1986 and 1988 is the pope's thinking about women in relation to family responsibilities. The 1986 encyclical, while arguing that men should play their part in family life, placed a much greater emphasis on the mothering role of women in the family, in no way paralleled by a fatherly role of men. *Mulieris dignitatem*, however, clearly affirms the necessity of both parents' taking responsibility for a child's upbringing. This is essential, *Mulieris dignitatem* insists, if marriage and family life are to reflect, as they should, the mystery of generation founded in God who is both mother and father of all creation.

20. Cahill, L. S., 'Sex and gender: the Universal Catechism's presentation', *America*, 162, 8 (1990), p. 60.

Reactions to the Teaching

Both René Coste and Lisa Sowle Cahill maintain that *Mulieris dignitatem's* attempt to change the concept of family care as 'women's work' is an important feature of its contribution to social and theological reflections on the issue.[21] In doing this, the document challenges universal assumptions about gender classifications within the family, models that have dictated expectations, behaviours, attitudes and motivations 'appropriate' to males or females.

Again there is an intersection between the arguments of the theological and secular feminist scholars and *Mulieris dignitatem*; for the issue of co-responsibility for children and the family has been a strong theme in contemporary feminist literature over recent decades.[22]

In these four areas, then – the affirmation of women's intrinsic equality to men, the naming of male domination as a consequence of the rupturing of humanity's relationship with God, the condemnation of any type of abuse and objectification of women by men, and the mutual responsibilities of parents for child-raising and family life – the document offers much encouragement and hope to women and men who are working for the conversion in heart and mind of those of the world and church who seek to justify structures that unjustly oppress women.

However, given that the document states that the Marian theme will be the unifying focus of its presentation, the Marian theme is also the focus of the document's critics. This same criticism can be levelled at *The Catechism of the Catholic Church* and *Ordinatio sacerdotalis*.

21. Cahill, L.S., 'Notes on moral theology: 1989, feminist ethics', *Theological Studies*, 51 (1990), p. 58; Coste, R., 'La lettre apostolique *Mulieris dignitatem* de Jean Paul II sur la dignité et la vocation de la femme', pp. 618f.
22. For a survey of the literature in this area see N. Chodrow, *The Reproduction of Mothering*, Berkeley, CA: University Press, 1978; H. Einstein, *Contemporary Feminist Thought*, London: Unwin, 1984; A. Rich, *Motherhood as Experience and Institution*, New York: W. W. Norton, 1976.

Commentators have challenged not just John Paul's mariology, but also the social and philosophical assumptions out of which it comes.

Mariology and Pope John Paul II

The main line of *Mulieris dignitatem's* teaching and the context for its entire reflection on women is to reflect simultaneously on Mary and her role in the life of the church. If one phrase could sum up this meditation regarding women finding their true vocation in the church and in the world it would be: Make Mary your model.

This presentation of Mary as model comes from Paul VI's *Marialis cultus*, which, as we noted in chapter one, lays an important foundation for *Mulieris dignitatem's* mariology. However, *Mulieris dignitatem* moves away from critical aspects of *Marialis cultus* and presents a more classical mariology.[23] Throughout *Mulieris dignitatem*, Mary is presented as the virgin mother, offering herself in fully graced freedom to be the mediatrix of salvation. Mary now reigns as Mother of God. Mary becomes a paradigm for all women.

Many of the commentators on the meditation do not find in its presentation of Mary an example they can relate to, nor can they perceive themselves through the mariology of it presents. In fact, Jackie Latham argues that this image is oppressive and an androcentric reinforcement of male stereotypes of women.[24]

Consequently, in spite of its many positive points, *Mulieris dignitatem* is criticized for presenting Mary as an impossible ideal for women. The impossibility of her example lies in the traditional way she is presented as both mother and yet virgin. This is something no

---

23. Paul VI believed that Mary was more a model for all people. He also argued that Marian devotion should be biblically based, reflective of the Christian themes, be in harmony with the liturgy and show an awareness of ecumenical concerns. See *Marialis cultus*, sect. 32.

24. Latham, J., 'Male and female He created them, not masculine and feminine', *The Month*, 22 (1989), p. 386.

woman can achieve. In the document's attempting to define the role of women through the role and example of Mary, some commentators maintain that an injustice is done to women because it speaks neither to their personal reality nor to the demands of their social and ethical situation today.

In fact the specific character of the statement's mariology has been attached by some to the experience of the pope. Peter Hebblethwaite has pointed out that the Polish pope's contribution to mariology over the last ten years has been distinctive. 'Having no sisters and never having seen his mother in good health and losing her altogether when he was nine predisposed him towards idealizing the feminine element in Mary'.[25] Added to this is the national Polish fervour given to Mary, Queen of Poland, whom the pope has addressed as 'Queen of social justice'. 'All of this makes for an extremely powerful cocktail of emotions', says Peter Hebblethwaite.

Interestingly, in *The Catechism of the Catholic Church* Mary is presented as a model for all Christians: '... from the church he [sic] learns the example of holiness and recognizes its model and source in the all-holy Virgin Mary.' However, in *Ordinatio sacerdotalis* John Paul II maintains that owing to the life of Mary and those women of the tradition who have followed her example, women have the model they need to 'become fully aware of the greatness of their mission'.

This is one area, then, where the interests of feminist scholars and papal reflection seem starkly divergent. Mainstream feminist mariology does not want to disregard Mary, but wants to 'liberate' her from the distortions of the classical Catholic tradition. It is Third World women who are leading the way. 'It is incumbent on the church of the poor, which is embodied today in the course taken by the base communities, to reflect ever more on the person and

25. Hebblethwaite, P., 'The mariology of the three Popes', *The Way Supplement*, 51 (1984), p. 63.

mystery of Mary within its context of oppression, struggle, resistance and victory.[26] 'Far from the spotless virgin of a male mariology, feminist biblical scholars are reclaiming 'the virgin betrothed and seduced or raped ... who conceives and bears the child they will call Emmanuel ... That Mary represents the oppressed who have been liberated.'[27]

Therefore Mary, for women, does not become an example of passive obedience who is vindicated by God, but an image of independence, a negation of the myth of feminine evil and a rejection of religion's fall into servitude to patriarchy.

Mary, in the history of Catholicism particularly, they maintain, has been given 'a necessary and praiseworthy role in the divine economy, but still it is a woman's role: auxiliary, subordinate, marked by emotionalism, irrationality, sensuality and ultimately, a lack of dignity'.[28]

Masculinity and femininity

One of the characteristics of *Mulieris dignitatem's* mariology is the distinction it makes between masculinity and femininity. It says that in the created order God intended a division in human nature to correspond to the individual genders of male and female. Mary is, for women, the archetype of the feminine nature. In and through her, all women come to discover their own nature as God intended it to be from the beginning. In Jesus' life this feminine nature is endorsed and promoted. The women who followed Jesus closely all had a de-

26. Gebara, I. & Bingemer, M., *Mary, Mother of God, Mother of the Poor*, Maryknoll NY: Orbis, 1989, p. 169.

27. Schaberg, J., 'The foremothers and the mother of Jesus', *Concilium*, 206 (1990), p. 118-119.

28. McLaughlin, E. C., 'Equality of souls; inequality of souls; inequality of sexes: woman in medieval theology', in R. Ruether (ed), *Religion and Sexism*, New York: Simon & Schuster, 1974, p. 250.

veloped sense of their unique femininity. It is this feminine response which enabled them to respond so fully to Jesus' needs and actions.

As a result of Mary's example and Jesus' activity toward women displaying this trait, it follows that all Christian women have a vocation to deepen their feminine characteristics. In fact, the protection of the distinctiveness between the masculine and feminine response to God is a crucial element of the church's mission in the world and a constitutive element in its anthropology. For just as the masculine and the feminine complement and explain each other, so too does Christ the groom complement and explain the church, his bride. Further still, the example of many women in the history of the church is that the deeper the ability to respond out of one's nature is, the deeper a life of holiness is attained.

This summary of the document's position on the complementarity question is deficient because what is meant is never clearly defined. Only in looking at the life of Mary, the women disciples of Jesus and the great women saints of the church, can a picture be drawn of the specific characteristics that relate to being feminine and, conversely, being masculine.

However, the distinctive complementarity which the document presumes in its exposition, has become the ground of significant criticism. Jackie Latham maintains that the document's use of masculine and feminine traits can be ascribed to the philosophy of nineteenth century positivism. Latham explains that during the last century, there grew up an idea that the some male characteristics are fundamentally opposed to a woman's nature. This arose out of the huge advances in the science of anatomy in that century, where the physical differences between men and women in bone structure, muscle fibre and reproductive process were investigated and catalogued. 'The problem with this view,' she says, 'is that anatomical and physiological differences are called on to determine the socially and culturally conditioned roles that have been assigned to the two sexes.'[29] The legacy of this nineteenth century movement is that sociological phenomena involved in role classification are referred to and seemingly endorsed by nature.

Other writers who agree with Latham's general thesis contend that the area where this distinction in *Mulieris dignitatem* is most significant is in its reflection on whether women can be presiders at the eucharist.[30] Here the document argues that the physical fact of maleness presents a 'clear and unambiguous [sign] when the sacramental ministry of the eucharist, in which the priest acts *in persona Christi*, is performed by a man'.

In summary, the document defends a distinction of ontological gender characteristics that is opposed to the consensus of contemporary feminist scholarly opinion. The argument of these scholars is that women and men have been socialized into gender roles and hierarchies. Far from these roles, functions, dispositions and characteristics that relate to men (the masculine) and women (the feminine) being a consequence of natural or divine ordering, this distinction and the accompanying gender organization in western civilization has been done to legitimate unjust power and dominance.[31]

Motherhood and virginity

Mulieris dignitatem, *Ordinatio sacerdotalis* and all papal teaching from Leo XIII to Pius XII, present motherhood as the fullest expression of a woman's vocation, precisely because it reflects the creativity

---

29. Latham, J., 'Male and female ...', p. 385.
30. Hebblethwaite, M., 'The Pope seems more conservative than misogynist', *National Catholic Reporter* , 25 (November, 1988), p. 15; Summerton, O., 'Pope John Paul ...', p. 221. For a full discussion of the other church documents that employ this same gender complementarity distinction, see S. Callahan, 'Person and gender, quelle différence?', *Church*, 6 (1990), pp. 5-9.
31. For a full discussion on the principles involved in gender role definitions in religion, see McGuire, M., *Religion: The Social Context*, pp. 89-104.

and generativity of God. Motherhood is a participation in the divine. *Mulieris dignitatem* can find no better example in the world of humanity's sharing in the partnership of creation with God than that of being a physical mother. Women were intended by God for this task and so are biologically equipped for this unique mission. Although it argues strongly for the co-responsibility of both mother and father in the task of parenting, it does accord the mother of a child a special role. As a result of carrying and bearing a baby, it states, a special communion exists between mother and child.

In every sense of this description, Mary, the mother of Jesus, is the prototype. She is also the mother of Christian faith and in this fulfils the characteristics outlined above: the fullest expression of human cooperation with God, created for the very purpose of bringing forth Jesus, and in so doing enjoying both a special communion with him, and through him also sharing a special intimacy with all humanity.

Mary also stands as the prototype of women's other vocational choice, virginity. For just as her maternity is all embracing, so too her virginity enables her to be fulfilled only by the love of Christ and the mission of his kingdom. This is the path of those women who freely choose celibacy for the sake of Christ. In doing so, though they may sacrifice physical motherhood, they take on motherhood in the spirit, begetting in those to whom they minister the gift of new life in Christ. Consequently, they are fulfilled by the love of Christ expressed in their spiritual maternity.

The document has been strongly challenged for these two options it presents to women. Critics have claimed that its treatment of motherhood and virginity is inadequate and out of touch with the reality of Christian women's lives.[32] Lisa Sowle Cahill contends that the essential problem is methodological. She states

---

32. For a full discussion of the many reactions, see Elizabeth Schüssler Fiorenza & Anne Carr (eds), 'Motherhood', *Concilium*, 206 (1990).

that *Mulieris dignitatem* never criticizes the context out of which the institution of motherhood has evolved. Consequently it has not addressed itself to the dominance of patriarchy in shaping and defining both the role and the activity of motherhood and virginity. The reason for this failure to be critical of the social context is clear to her: 'Women's embodiment and motherhood as experience and as institution are ... crucial to a number of specific ethical dilemmas, preeminently abortion and reproductive technologies'.[33] Therefore, she argues, the teaching church has a significant investment in arguing the case it does for motherhood in *Mulieris dignitatem*

Other commentators have focused on how Mary is used as an example of motherhood. Johanna Kohn-Roelin charges that while motherhood is seen by this document as the great task of human 'entrusting', especially in the way it upholds the example of the mother of Jesus, it 'does not mean that women are offered any correspondingly important liturgical service or ordination to the ministries...Publicly the ideal of 'being a mother' is loaded with sentiment whereas in reality, society [religious society included] exploits mothers'.[34]

Women who are physical mothers have not been the only group to criticize the document for its presentation of their particular vocation. Religious women have done so too. These women, of whom South American theologian, Ivone Gebara is representative, are referred to in the document as spiritual mothers. Gebara addresses herself to the entire Catholic tradition when she observes that the history of spiritual motherhood has been defined and control-

---

33. Cahill L. S., 'Feminist ethics ', p. 61.
34. Kohn-Roelin J., 'Mother-daughter-God', *Concilium*, 206 (1990), p. 66.
35. Gebara, I., 'The mother superior and spiritual motherhood: from intuition to institution', *Concilium*, 206 (1990), p. 44.

led by an 'androcentric and theocentric view of the universe and also by a deeply dualist view of human nature'.[35] Gebara does not wish to dispense with the concept or lived experience of spiritual motherhood, but wants it understood in a new light. For her, the women of the Third World, widows, married and single parents who have experienced the pain of suffering, who alleviate the 'orphanhood' of the men and women who are facing oppression, torture and death, lead the way in helping the church understand this vocation. 'We have seen that true "spiritual motherhood", the sort that really helps life to burst forth, has leaped over the walls of the institution and shown that the gift of begetting the life in the Spirit cannot be contained in prefabricated or carefully guarded models.'

Gregory Baum contends that in proposing only two choices for women the document excludes single professional women, who do not feel drawn to vows of chastity, poverty and obedience. He observes, 'While John XXIII regarded the active presence of women in public life as part of the sign of the times, the Letter does not pursue this line of thought. Indeed, if the Blessed Virgin Mary sums up the vocation of womanhood their participation in society as thinkers, inventors, initiators, presiders and leaders is hardly part of the divinely appointed destiny of women. Such a position would be wholly unacceptable to contemporary men and women'.[36]

The ordination of women

Mulieris dignitatem turns its attention to the issue of women's ordination for only one section, three pages in all. Although this issue receives such a small treatment, the document does not indicate that it is of minor importance. The fact is that, for the past two decades,

---

36. Baum, G. 'Bulletin ...', p.147.

the whole debate over this subject has escalated rather than subsided, even in the face of official statements that the issue of women's ordination was now closed.[37]

Given this situation, *Mulieris dignitatem* summarizes in a few pages what the Congregation for the Doctrine of the Faith said in 1976. The Congregation concluded that 'it is necessary to recall that the church, in fidelity to the example of the Lord, does not consider herself authorized to admit women to priestly ordination'.[38] It cited six reasons why this was the case:

— the church had never had women priests;
— Christ did not call any woman to be one of the twelve apostles;
— the twelve followed in the practice of Jesus and ordained only men to the priesthood;
— this apostolic example has been regarded by the church as normative and therefore the desire of Christ for the church;
— the priest must be male, so as to be the *persona Christi*;
— the formula of Galatians 3:28 does not refer to gender inclusion in ministries but 'only affirms the universal calling to divine filiation, which is the same for all'.

Mulieris dignitatem places the whole question within the ecclesial perspective of the Bride of Christ (the church) being faithful to

37. It is interesting to note that Pope John Paul said in the early 1980s that the issue of women's ordination was definitively closed and yet in *Mulieris dignitatem* responded again to the objections against the church's stance. He repeated, in the strongest possible terms, that the non-admittance of women to ordination 'is to be definitively held by all the church's faithful'. See *Ordinatio sacredotalis*, sect. 4.

38. Sacred Congregation for the Doctrine of the Faith, *Declaration on the questions of the admission of women to the ministerial priesthood*, Sydney: St Pauls Publications, 1976, sect. 5.

the Spouse (Christ). It argues that this relationship between groom and bride is consummated at the celebration of the eucharist; consequently the role of each partner needs be 'clear and unambiguous'. It rejects the argument that developed in response to the Declaration of the Congregation, that Jesus chose men as a consequence of his cultural/historical limitations, by stating that 'Christ acted in a completely free and sovereign manner'. This contribution to the discussion has been welcomed by some scholars and lay people as timely, crucial and necessary.

Many other people, however, have attacked the document's stand on this issue and charged that its rationale, on this point, is what Gregory Baum calls one of 'the redeeming inconsistencies in the letter'. For while the document venerates motherhood, be it in physical or spiritual terms, as partaking in God's generativity, it also seems to believe that 'potential motherhood, which is the genius of women, makes them unfit for ordination'.[39]

Irish theologian Dominic O'Laoghaire argues that by using the bride of Christ analogy in defending a male priesthood, more difficulties are created than are resolved. He believes that when the

---

39. In my opinion, Hans von Balthasar's argument for the Christian concept of motherhood is the source for the meditation's position. He argued that the church was possibly the last community to have a 'genuine appreciation of the difference between the sexes'. He protested that 'every encroachment of one sex into the role of the other narrows the range and dynamics of humanly possible love'. This point was observable for him in the life of the church, in how Mary is called Queen of the Apostles, 'without claiming apostolic powers for herself. She possesses something else and something more.' The something more and the something else is motherhood, the feminine principle of 'active fruitfulness which is already superior to that of the man'. Hence, what is true for Mary is true for all women, that is, motherhood is a higher calling than that to be priest, which is 'appropriation as expropriation; leadership, but from the last place'. Mulieris dignitatem agrees entirely with von Balthasar's theology on this point. See H. von Balthasar, 'Women Priests?', *New Elucidations*, San Francisco: Ignatius Press, 1986, pp. 192-196.

analogy is pushed to its logical conclusion, if the priest appears to be standing in at the eucharist for the male bridegroom, and the people (both men and women) are the bride, then the gains of the church's struggle to celebrate Christ's unity of divinity and humanity are in danger. 'Do we not risk ... some over-emphasis on the humanity of Christ, especially on his male humanity, as against his divinity?'[40] Second, the bride of Christ model presumes an image of patriarchal marriage, where the bride waits on the groom for all his needs. This goes against the mutual relationship that the document advocates in marriage elsewhere. O'Laoghaire notes here that some men find it very difficult to hear themselves talked about as being 'in the Bride', waiting for eucharistic intimacy with Christ the groom.

Finally, at least one writer argues that the whole model in *Mulieris dignitatem* raises the question of whether a male saviour can save women. 'If women cannot represent a male redeemer, it would seem to follow that a male redeemer cannot represent women ... It would mean women have never been redeemed!'[41]

In the wider debate on women acting *in persona Christi*, which has been a constant topic since the publication of the Declaration in 1977, writers have been critical of how the teaching office of the church appropriates and understands the maleness of Jesus in Christian theology. What has been said in recent years on this issue is most pertinent to our discussion here, for *Mulieris dignitatem* reiterates the same position of previous statements. No one in the mainstream of this debate questions the historical fact of Jesus' biological male gender. The division in the debate occurs in understanding that historical fact and its continuing revelation in the symbolic life of the church. Baum posits that sometimes so much emphasis is placed on Jesus' maleness that the question arises whether 'male genitals are a

---

40. O'Laoghaire, D., 'The dignity of women', *Doctrine and Life*, 39 (1989) p. 78.
41. Hebblethwaite, M., 'The Pope seems more conservative than misogynist'.

requirement for priesthood' and whether this defines 'what is meant by *persona Christi*'.[42] Writers on the issue of the relationship between Jesus' maleness and women's exclusion from the priesthood have not all been women who seek to be ordained. George Worgul, in an important article on the anthropological presumptions behind this argument, concludes, 'If the eucharistic presider symbolizes Christ, especially in speaking the words of consecration, it is the peace, love and justice which constitute Jesus' mission and ministry and actualize his personhood as revealer and saviour which attain primary signification and not Jesus' bio-physiological maleness.'[43]

Ordinatio sacerdotalis, curiously, does not mention the argument from the icon of Christ, so strongly developed in *Mulieris dignitatem*, but restates the Declaration's central position that women cannot be admitted to the priesthood because Christ chose only men to be his apostles.

Conclusion

Most of the commentators agree that very real advances are made in *Mulieris dignitatem* on a number of critical issues. These are:

— that the discussion of women's rights has only clouded the underlying need for all people to recognize women's dignity;

— that women are intrinsically equal to men, created so by God in God's image and likeness;

— that the domination of women by men is one of the clearest signs of the disordered relationship humanity has with God as a result of sin;

— that any abuse of women by men is not only destructive for

---

42. Baum, G., 'Bulletin ...', p. 148.
43. Worgul, G. S., 'Ritual, power, authority and riddles: the anthropology of Rome's declaration on the ordination of women', *Louvain Studies*, 14 (1989), p. 58.

women, but is also negative for all;

— that the parenting of children and the care of the home
should be a task which both women and men share in
equally.

Conversely, commentators have nominated several areas in the
document with which they disagree and from which they subse-
quently dissent. They are:

— that the classical mariology presented in the document
promotes an impossible ideal for women to live up to, and
blurs the model Jesus provides for all people;

— that the contingent discussion of the gender
complementarity distinctions within the mariology of
the document is based on questionable philosophical and
scientific theory;

— that the categories of motherhood and virginity, as
described in the document, are too restrictive and out of
touch with the experience of the majority of women who
are presently living out these vocations;

— that the restatement of women's exclusion from the
priesthood brings into focus an unnecessary attachment,
theologically, to the importance of Jesus' maleness for the
one who is to act *in persona Christi*.

There is an underlying connection between these criticisms.
It is this: in each case where *Mulieris dignitatem* has been judged to
be questionable, writers have generally maintained that the document should have been more critical of the context out of which
the theological issue, social institution, gender distinction or power
presumptions have arisen. In doing this, *Mulieris dignitatem* would
have needed to have been self-critical, demonstrating the church's
culpability in regard to discrimination against women.

However, the lack of self-criticism is not only the unifying principle in the commentaries of the document's detractors, it is also the key to understanding why it argues the way it does. The issue at stake here is not sociological or theological, but methodological. This concern is not purely with the construction of its argumentation but more with the methodology that is at the heart of its thesis. In this document's exposition on women's status and role, one finds papal ecclesiology in theory and in practice.

For any meaningful dialogue to occur between the parties involved in the debate on the status and activity of women in the church, a clear recognition of the personal presumptions, theological starting points and socio-political goals of each participant, including the teaching office of the church, will have to be recognized publicly.

Part four

*Interpreting the sources:
papal versus feminist
hermeneutics*

Chapter 5

The Hermeneutics of Pope John Paul II

WHY IS IT THAT THE PEOPLE involved in the discussion on women's dignity and vocation cannot come to some greater degree of consensus? I believe that the essential problem is hermeneutical, that is, one of interpretation.[44] For this reason, the focus on the theological detail in papal teaching displaces the real conflict. The essential problem lies in how interested parties in the debate appropriate, comprehend and interpret the sources of Christian tradition in relation to women from their own perspectives and in response to the demands of their own worldview.

We need to explore papal hermeneutics, the environment of interpretation out of which papal documents are written. This requires an analysis of popes in general, and John Paul II in particular, appropriate and employ the scriptural record and theological tradition in such documents.

To provide some contrast to this approach, we will also analyze the hermeneutical approach of biblical scholar Elisabeth Schüssler

---

44. 'Hermeneutics' is used here in the sense of the theory and practice of interpretation. More precisely it is understood in terms of Paul Ricoeur's theory that the story (scriptures), symbols, traditions, art or doctrine of any group give rise to truth that can be uncovered by philosophical interpretation. See Ricoeur P., 'Hermeneutics' in J. O. Ree & J. O. Urmson (eds), *The Concise Encyclopedia of Western Philosophy*, London: Unwin Hyman, 1989.

Fiorenza. Fiorenza has emerged as the leading and most influential figure in Christian feminist hermeneutical inquiry in the last decade. She is also concerned with the same issues that are addressed by the popes. Consequently, a comparison between her approach and that of the document highlights effectively the dramatically different rules for interpretation that render such diverse readings of the same material and history.

Rather than keep this discussion in the abstract, we will analyze the implications of these two approaches by turning to chapter nine of *Mulieris dignitatem*, 'Jesus Christ'. This chapter provides excellent material in which to observe the differences between papal and feminist hermeneutics. Both *Mulieris dignitatem* and Elisabeth Schüssler Fiorenza have gone to extraordinary lengths to respectively establish, understand and interpret the relationship Jesus Christ has with women today. Further, we have drawn attention throughout this work to the common thread which *Mulieris dignitatem* states is at the centre of its reflections, namely the special place of the 'Mother of Christ' in reflecting on the vocation and dignity of women.

The question remains then, if Mary is the model for women, what is their relationship to Jesus? *Mulieris dignitatem* addresses this question in chapter nine, so it is fitting that, in taking this chapter as a case study in the contrasting schools of hermeneutics at work, it should also elucidate the pope's position on this critical issue.

Papal hermeneutics

While it is true that *Mulieris dignitatem* fulfils all the criteria of the status of an apostolic letter and as a result makes a consequent claim of assent, it still remains qualitatively different in style to all other papal documents about women. This difference is quite intentional and is made explicit in the introduction to the letter. There the pope writes that, given the context of the Marian Year and the broad scope of the subject about to be pursued, 'it seems to me that the best thing is to give this text the style and character of a meditation'.

A meditation as such is an unknown official category for a papal pronouncement. Its definition in recent Christian usage means that it is a spiritual recollection of an exposition on the truths of Christian faith that is offered for people to pray over and reflect on in their own lives. Consequently, *Mulieris dignitatem* is like an extended homily, a form of literary discourse that, while well ordered and logical, offers pastoral reflections and suggestions rather than detailed exegesis or theologizing. As a homily, it draws its authority not so much from the claims of scholarship as from an appeal to experience and reflection – papal experience, both personal and in the tradition. A homily is also a passive form of discourse. An appointed person speaks and the congregation, in Catholic churches anyway, remains silent.

If the document is a meditation, then it is explicitly hermeneutical. It interprets the events and reflections of the Christian tradition by meditating on their meaning today. It is not exegesis or systematic theologizing as such, but an authoritative, but not definitive, pastoral homily.

Mulieris dignitatem states that the focus of the meditation is a 'further study of the anthropological and theological bases that are needed in order to solve the problem connected with the meaning and dignity of being a woman and being a man'. Apart from this being a difficult task for a homily, the question arises whether the exclusively male teaching office of the Roman Catholic Church is competent to explore the bases of being a woman.

It is this important question that provides the focus for our brief inquiry into the rationale of papal hermeneutics. The fact is that popes have obviously seen themselves well placed to offer reflections on the dignity and vocation of women, because they understand the entire issue to be one within the domain of ecclesiology. 'The

Second Vatican Council, confirming the teaching of the whole [my emphasis] of tradition, recalled that in the hierarchy of holiness it is precisely 'the woman, Mary of Nazareth, who is the figure of the church ... In this sense, one can say that the church is both Marian and Apostolic-Petrine ... this same thing is repeated down the centuries from one generation to the next, as the history of the church demonstrates.'

The popes have understood this task of teaching on the life of women and their essential qualities as a way of being faithful to the example of Christ. *Mulieris dignitatem*, for example, takes to itself the mission given to the apostles during Jesus' public life (Matthew 10:1-42; Luke 9:1-10) and after the resurrection (Matthew 28:18-20; Mark 16: 15-18), the assurance of the Holy Spirit in preaching and teaching the Word (Matthew 28:20; John 14:15-19, 26, 15:26-27, 16:12-14; Luke 24:48; Acts 1:8) and the authority of this mission as a revelation of the essential truths of salvation (Acts 2:42, 4:32-33, 5:12-13, 1 Timothy 6:20-21; 2 Timothy 1:13-4). This is presumed in its hermeneutic, for, just as Jesus spoke of women and knew what was 'in them', so too the teaching office of the church, in all its teaching function, sees itself as the authoritative witness to the apostolic charge.[45]

Added to this teaching mission is the concept of continuing to guard the deposit of faith. In other words, papal teaching presumes an acceptance of the fact that it is best placed to interpret and transmit the essential christian truths as they have been handed down from the end of the apostolic era, through the centuries to

---

45. Dulles, A., *The Catholicity of the Church*, Oxford: Clarendon Press, 1985, pp. 138ff. Also see J. L. McKenzie, *Authority in the Church*, New York: Sheed & Ward, 1966; J. Ratzinger, *Principles of Catholic Theology*, San Francisco: Ignatius Press, 1987, chap. 2; *Lumen Gentium, Documents of Vatican II*, A. Flannery (ed.), New York: Costello, sects.18 & 19.

the present pope. In so far as the whole church continues to be an authentic bearer of Christ's truth, then it is presumed that whenever the leader of this universal community teaches, such teaching will be an appropriate witness, continuation and application of the truth Jesus preached and commissioned the apostles to proclaim.

In terms of the scope of *Mulieris dignitatem*, then, papal hermeneutics understands that the anthropological and theological bases of being a man and a woman are well within its apostolic brief. In fact, it is its apostolic responsibility to interpret and define what it understands as woman's essential character, as Christ proclaimed it, in the face of the contemporary movement for women's rights which threatens to deform women of their 'feminine originality ... which constitutes their essential richness'.

Scripture and tradition;

So far, then, we have established two principles of papal hermeneutics: first, the starting point for papal teaching is rooted in understanding that the duty and right to teach comes from Christ and is a function performed on behalf of, and in, the church; second, actual teaching, such as in *Mulieris dignitatem*, is a continuation of this apostolic ministry, an extension and application of it for our present day.

In the light of these starting points, scripture and tradition are appropriated. The papal approach to scripture is to understand that it belongs to the church and, consequently, its interpretation is always done most authentically within the church community. When new and variant interpretations of scriptural passages arise, they are judged against the traditional and usually long-standing understanding of the text and its social and theological implications. The myriad forms of historical-critical methodologies, reader-interaction theories, or new schools of scriptural hermeneutics are scrutinized through the lens of the whole sense of scripture expressed within the whole Christian community.

Examples of this approach in action are found in *Mulieris dignitatem* and *Ordinatio sacerdotalis*, where John Paul II dismisses new interpretations of Jesus' being culturally bound in choosing twelve male apostles. These documents reassert the traditional view that Jesus transcends cultural norms by citing how free Jesus was in relation to his way of acting elsewhere in the gospels. The assumption here is that Jesus would be consistent in action. If, in Luke for example, Jesus is a friend of the leper or outcast, a socially outrageous activity, then in Matthew, Mark or John, it can not be true that Jesus reverts to cultural limitations in regard to choosing his apostles. In this way the long line of apostolic continuity and interpretation is seen to safeguard the relationship between scripture and the community and the scriptural record itself from false interpretations.

This way of proceeding with scripture is vital in understanding papal teaching on women. Most of the critics of this teaching do not take these documents on their own scriptural terms, and therefore they demand of them to be an example of biblical exegetical methodology. For papal hermeneutics, however, functional specialities, like exegesis, are useful in contributing to the understanding of the whole sense of scripture, but equally their validity is judged by the whole Christian community.

For example, if we take *Mulieris dignitatem* seriously as a meditation – an extended homily – then it must be recognized that scriptural interpretation has a special and specific role in homiletics. A homily, as complex and erudite as it might be, is basically modelling the gospels themselves, which are homiletic documents – telling the story of Jesus for their audience, given their communities' particular historical situation. This is precisely what *Mulieris dignitatem* is doing. It is retelling the story of the Christian church in relation to the particular situation of women, drawing on the whole community's experience and reflection on the life of Jesus and the example of Mary.

What we need to take note of here is that scriptural interpretation in papal documents is not simply applied exegesis; what is at issue is a whole ecclesiology. Until we come to understand how scripture is appropriated in this ecclesiology we will not be able to adequately comprehend the relationship between scripture, apostolic authority and continuity, proclamation and tradition. These are premises of scriptural hermeneutics in papal documents on women.

Papal hermeneutics, as well as having this nuanced approach to scripture, has a similar approach to tradition. In fact, to make distinctions in regard to scripture, tradition and teaching authority is somewhat artificial, for papal hermeneutics rests on a premise of unity between them: 'It is clear that sacred tradition, sacred scripture and the teaching authority of the church, in accord with God's most wise design, are so linked and joined together that one cannot stand without the other, and that all together and each in its own way under the action of the one Holy Spirit contribute effectively to the salvation of souls'.[46]

Scripture itself is seen to be the product of tradition, thereby establishing an authority and status for tradition that is not only intrinsic to the essence of the church, but also to the essence of humanity.[47] Tradition, in the papal school, and as can be clearly seen in all papal teaching on women, is not just a matter of passing on the insights and rituals of previous generations, but also a matter of 'sifting out the truth of the Christian witness from the distortions of human blindness and ignorance. It has a corrective as well as an interpretative function.'[48]

---

46. Ratzinger, J., *Principles of Catholic Theology*, pp. 86ff.
47. *Dei verbum*, 'Dogmatic Constitution on Divine Revelation', Vatican II, sect.10.
48. Dulles, A., *The Catholicity of the Church*, pp. 103f.

To show the role tradition plays in papal hermeneutics and to establish the basis for the analysis of chapter nine of *Mulieris dignitatem*, a very brief survey of the document's presumptions in regard to christology is instructive.

Throughout *Mulieris dignitatem* Jesus is presented in what has come to be termed as a high christology. This means that the presumption rests on Jesus' divinity, that Jesus is 'first and foremost the second person of the Trinity – the divine *logos* in human form'.[49] This is the usual starting point for papal documents, taking the christology of the fourth gospel as their basis.

Implicit in the christology of *Mulieris dignitatem* are a number of factors that rest on tradition. These are:

— the beliefs that Christ is the definitive self-revelation of God;

— that this self- revelation is made within the life (tradition) of the Christian community;

— that the scriptures crystallize this self-revelation;

— that therefore Christ is only truly known through the life (tradition) of the church;

- that therefore the suggestions about the historical Jesus and his relationship to women are tested by the living Christ in the church;

— that therefore christology and ecclesiology are again inseparable.

It follows, then, that papal christology rests on how thinking about Jesus developed through tradition. Under the guidance of the Holy Spirit, it is accepted that historical interpretations about Jesus

---

49. Gomas, F., 'Christology and pastoral practice from below', *East Asian Pastoral Review*, vol. 1 (1982), p. 5; Also see E. Johnson, *Consider Jesus*, New York: Crossroads, 1990, pp. 36-38.

offer the truth about God's activity in and through Christ. Only through prayer and faith can one appropriate the most authentic picture of Jesus Christ and this is done best by the church through reflecting on tradition. Consequently, it follows that any process or methodology which wants to disregard tradition or neutralize it is dismissed. For in studying the person and work of Jesus Christ the task is not merely a theological one, but, as Joseph Ratzinger concludes, the study of the God-man leads to 'humanity's humanization'.[50] Therefore one's approach to christology and one's subsequent conclusions are most serious and onerous tasks.

Conclusions

We have now identified four general elements of papal hermeneutics — the mission of Jesus given to the church to teach in his name; the continuation of the apostolic ministry of defending and promoting the essential Christian truths; the citing of scriptural interpretation as a function within the whole church; and tradition as guardian of truth about humanity as a whole, not just the deposit of Christian doctrine. It is out of this context that the teaching office of the church approaches the subject of the 'anthropological and theological bases of what it means to be a woman' and 'meditates' on them.

---

50. Ratzinger, J., *Principles of Catholic Theology*, p.101.

Chapter 6

The approach of Elisabeth Schüssler Fiorenza

WE BEGAN THIS SECTION by drawing attention to the significant hermeneutical problems that presently block constructive dialogue about women's issues in the Roman Catholic Church. The essential problem lies in how various people approach and interpret the scriptural and traditional sources of Christianity in relation to women from their own worldviews.

We now turn to Elisabeth Schüssler Fiorenza as one example of a scholar who is grappling with the same sources, the biblical narrative and the church's theological history, but who brings to these sources a completely different hermeneutic from the papal one and consequently reads them in a dramatically contrasting way. Fiorenza is not on her own as a woman scholar attempting to interpret the status and mission of women from Christian traditions. In fact there have emerged in the last twenty years three major schools of biblical, as well as theological, criticism from feminist perspectives. A brief outline of each of them will provide a background to Fiorenza's work, for she borrows aspects from two of them and works out of the third.

Phyllis Trible, in her two ground-breaking texts, *God and the Rhetoric of Sexuality* and *Texts of Terror*, established what has come to be termed as the revisionist approach to biblical and theological interpretation. Trible argues that although the texts of the Hebrew scriptures are intrinsically patriarchal, present within them, as well, is a 'depatriarchalizing principle'. This principle, present in significant texts, challenges the gender presumptions of the text and enables women to emerge from the biblical tradition in their own right. Consequently the scriptures are revised to recover the occasions where women can see their foresisters present as strong, independent women of faith used by God to challenge the gender presumptions of the time and culture. In turn, then, these texts become the 'biblical stories of terror in memoriam', the basis for women to reclaim their dignity and mission today.

The second school of Christian feminist theological criticism to emerge has been called liberationist. Rosemary Radford Ruether and Letty Russell are the leading exponents of this hermeneutic. While there are differences between these two scholars in practice, together they argue that the entire canon of scripture must be read in the light of God liberating all those oppressed by injustice. They hold that biblical texts, when read in this light, reveal God's rejection of socio-historical ordering of men over women and support the contemporary women's movement towards social and political equality with men. Ruether and Russell reject previous readings of biblical texts that find justification for patriarchy within them as the distortions of the so-called 'objective' biblical scholarship. They argue that no one reads the scriptures value free and that only in presenting one's agenda openly can the social reformation that they promise occur. In fact, it is the 'prophetic liberating tradition' of the scriptures which becomes the 'norm through which to criticise the Bible'. Out of this liberationist critical reading a 'useable tradition' emerges.

The third school of feminist biblical hermeneutics is the theological/reconstructionist school.[51] This is the school out of which

---

51. I am grateful to Elaine Wainwright for this category and terminology in her doctoral dissertation, 'Towards a feminist reading of the gospel of Matthew', University of Queensland, 1991, p. 19.

The Approach of Elisabeth Schüssler Fiorenza

Elisabeth Schüssler Fiorenza works. As the title suggests, it is primarily about reconstructing the situation of the early church which produced the gospels, so as to understand both the theology and historical reality contained therein. As Katherine Sakenfield observes, 'the goal of her work is to recover the non-patriarchal early Christian ethos as a basis for Christian theology'.[52]

Schüssler Fiorenza explicitly argues for a feminist critical theory of liberation, but unlike Ruether and Russell with their general interpretative principle, she believes that 'biblical texts must be considered within the particular book to which they belong'.[53] Fiorenza holds that the starting point for her theological/reconstructionist paradigm is recognition that the scriptural word has been used to discriminate against women. Consequently her approach calls for a re-evaluation and re-assessment of the authority of these texts. The new locus of authority rests in how much these texts hinder or support women in our struggle to end social and ecclesiastical patriarchy'.[54]

Feminist theological/reconstructionist hermeneutics

Out of this brief and all too simple reduction of Elizabeth Schüssler Fiorenza's starting points, we consider her approach to interpretation, through exploring the four elements of her procedure:

— a hermeneutic of suspicion;
— a hermeneutic of critical remembrance;

52. Sakenfield, K., 'Feminist perspectives on bible and theology', *Interpretation* (3) 1, (1989) p.7.
53. Wainwright, E., 'Towards a feminist reading of the gospel of Matthew', p. 21.
54. Fiorenza, E. S., 'Theological criteria and historical reconstruction: Martha and Mary: Luke 10:38-42', *Protocol of the Centre for Hermeneutical Studies*, 53, 1986, p. 2.

— a hermeneutic of proclamation;
— a hermeneutic of actualization and ritualization.

A hermeneutic of suspicion. This is the cornerstone of Fiorenza's hermeneutical edifice. It is what she terms a hermeneutic of suspicion rather than acceptance. It places on all texts the label 'Caution: could be dangerous to your health and survival.'[55] This foundation comes from her experience of feeling marginalized and dehumanized as a result of patriarchal abuse of the Bible and the theological tradition. Fiorenza argues this abuse of the Bible can be seen in the way women's anger and rebellion has been quietened by the androcentric interpretation of scriptural stories pertaining to women.

In essence, then, Fiorenza moves toward all biblical texts and theological traditions suspicious that the experience of women is not reflected or recorded in them. 'Revelation and theology are so intertwined that they can no longer be adequately distinguished ... [both] express truth in sexist language and images and participate in the myth of their patriarchal-sexist society and culture.'[56] Therefore, reading them in the light of feminist liberation involves unmasking the 'detached, neutral, scientific and unbiased scholarship' of the church and reveal that the tradition, far from displaying 'how it really was', demonstrates the politics in presenting 'how it shall be remembered'.[57]

A hermeneutic of remembrance. Suspicion of all scriptural and theological texts leads Fiorenza to ask further questions of the text and the historical situation that lies behind the text. Fiorenza states that this 'hermeneutic of critical remembrance and historical reconstruc-

---

55. Fiorenza, E. S., 'Theological criteria and historical reconstruction', p. 2.
56. Fiorenza, E. S., 'Feminist theology as a critical theology of liberation', *Theological Studies*, 36 (1975), p. 611.
57. Fiorenza, E. S., *Bread not Stone: The Challenge of Feminist Biblical Interpretation*, Boston: Beacon Press, 1984, p. 143.

tion ... traces the struggles of our foresisters'.[58] Citing the baptismal formulas of Galatians 2:27ff — in 'Christ Jesus there is neither Jew nor Greek, slave nor free, neither male nor female' — Fiorenza argues that the Christian church has fallen away from this imperative. Even though the official church continues to affirm the Christian community as one of equality in its *Constitution on the Church*, it has failed to live up to it with its praxis.

Fiorenza's task, then, is to reconstruct the feminist history of the first centuries of the Christian church's tradition and 'demonstrate how difficult it was for the ecclesial establishment to suppress the call and spirit of freedom among Christian women'. By doing so, Fiorenza reclaims the memory of the women of the New Testament, those known and those unknown, as well as the women of the tradition. 'A hermeneutic of remembrance reclaims their sufferings and struggles through the subversive power of the remembered past.'

To undertake this task, Fiorenza marshals three major discursive practices: historical and literary biblical criticism, liberation theologies and feminist critical theory. In applying them, she establishes a 'window to the world behind the text'.[59]

A hermeneutic of proclamation. 'Taken alone, this goal of theological reconstruction bears within it the inherent danger of the text becoming simply a window to the world in front of the text and the liberating vision it can present to the church of women.[60] 'To avoid this problem, Fiorenza advocates a hermeneutic of proclamation, which assesses the interaction between the scriptural text and the theological tradition and looks to the power this interaction has for the entire church.

---

58. Fiorenza, E. S., 'Theological criteria and historical reconstruction', p. 2.
59. Wainwright, E., 'Towards a feminist reading of the gospel of Matthew', p. 21.
60. ibid., p. 21.

The task of proclamation is all-encompassing. Fiorenza advocates a radical reading of tradition where the reader does not fasten on the past but becomes committed to God's vision of a new creation. Paradoxically this new creation is based on the historical example of Jesus and his discipleship of equals and so the *ekklesia* of women, she advocates, is mutual with men so that both genders reach their full potential as persons and disciples.

The implications of this hermeneutic of proclamation is that feminist theological enquiry also serves the interests of other political aspirants who are aligned with women seeking liberation from patriarchy in the church. Fiorenza outlines these people as those who seek an end to the global feminist movement in the social sphere, and an option for the oppressed wherever they may be and whatever situation in which they may find themselves. It is out of a common experience of otherness that the proclamation of women's liberation from Christian patriarchy enables them to embrace any women who is exploited or marginalized. 'Feminism's self-understanding and analysis must shift therefore from a preoccupation with gender dualism in order to attend to the interstructing of sex, race, class, culture, religion in systems of domination.'[61]

In Fiorenza's proclamation of liberation, Christian tradition and biblical witness is deconstructed and reconstructed in terms of 'a global praxis for liberation ... [a] politics of otherness inscribed in its [the Bible's] pages'.[62] In traditional theological language she proclaims a theology that demands conversion and repentance and a new mission and community.

A hermeneutic of actualization and ritualization. In the final category

---

61 Fiorenza E. S., 'The politics of otherness: biblical interpretation as a critical praxis for liberation', in *The Future of Liberation Theology*, M. H. Ellis & O. Madurano (eds) New York: Orbis, 1989, p. 316.

62. ibid., p. 317.

of Fiorenza's theological method, the role of 'historical imagination, artistic representation and liturgical celebration' is emphasized and explored.

Fiorenza argues that just as the patriarchal church has developed its tradition over the centuries through ritual, movement, gesture, word, art, music and story telling, so too Christian feminist theology must develop these capacities in its remembering, proclaiming and retelling of the story of women. For just as the task of theology and biblical criticism is to appeal to our rational senses, so too Fiorenza's approach provides for myths, symbols and rituals that 'encourage particular forms of behaviour and implicitly embody goals and value judgements'.[63] In her case, of course, the behaviour, goals and judgements would be those congruent with the feminist struggle for liberation. This area provides a significant meeting point between Fiorenza's and papal hermeneutics: the centrality of ritual for expression and internalization of intellectual concepts.

However, the manifestations of both approaches are significantly different. At the base of Fiorenza's model is an understanding that, at most, the tradition of church provides a prototype which we imitate, reinterpret or change. As we have seen, papal hermeneutics works from a strongly defined sense of the archetype that tradition holds and defends it in both the words of the scriptural record and the actions of Christian history.

Fiorenza encourages a search for new images, new myths which could 'incarnate the new vision of Christian women' that she observes is emerging. Of particular importance here is her call for women to reclaim themselves as the body of Christ and their bodies as the image of Christ. To that end she advocates imagination, art and ritual in communal liturgical actions. She states that the long-

---

63. Fiorenza, E. S., 'Feminist theology as a critical theology of liberation',
   p. 620.

term objective of this hermeneutic is to see women preside at the eucharist. 'As long as women Christians are excluded from breaking the bread and deciding their own spiritual welfare and commitment, *ekklesia*, as the discipleship of equals, is not realized and the power of God is greatly diminished.'[64]

---

64. Fiorenza E. S., *In Memory of Her: A Feminist Reconstruction of Christian Origins*, London: SCM Press, 1983, p. 24.

Chapter 7

Jesus and Women:
A Case Study of
Applied Hermeneutics

HAVING SET OUT TWO WAYS of interpretation: the papal approach and a feminist theological/reconstructionist approach, we will look at the way these theories and practices affect particular issues and texts. We will also analyze how each uses scripture in mounting a theological argument. We concentrate on two issues: the liberation Jesus brings to women and the mission Jesus gives women.

Why these two? Because both papal teaching and Elizabeth Schüssler Fiorenza believe that freedom in Christ and an active apostolic vocation are the primary hallmarks of Christian womanhood. However, their respective readings of the scriptural text render almost diametrically opposite interpretations of what constitutes and defines this freedom and gives direction and authority to this vocation.

Following closely the examples *Mulieris dignitatem* draws on in chapter nine, 'Jesus Christ', we will look first at Mary of Bethany in Luke's gospel and Martha in John's gospel as paradigms of Jesus' gift of liberation to women, and then look at Mary Magdalene in John's gospel as a paradigm of women's apostolic mission.

The liberation Jesus brings to women

In section 15, *Mulieris dignitatem* turns its attention to the implications of Jesus' activity in the socio-political world of first century Palestine. It says not only that Jesus' behaviour at the time was a protest against the discrimination women suffered, but that 'Christ's way of acting ... is a consistent protest'. In this way Jesus' behaviour is not forgotten but remembered by women today and through all ages. Consequently, they continue to 'feel liberated by this truth, restored to themselves: they feel loved with eternal love ... their position is transformed.'

This critical passage needs careful analysis. *Mulieris dignitatem* argues that this truth accomplishes four things: liberation, restoration, an experience of transcendent love and a transformation of women's actual social position. It attests how Jesus confronted unjust structures that oppressed women in his day and proclaimed freedom from them for his followers. Now, through the church, Christ continues to free women from oppression and restore their feminine dignity. This, then, is the first of the papal hermeneutical principles in action: establishing what the words and actions of Jesus were and then interpreting them in terms of an ongoing apostolic charge.

Women, liberated from 'the concrete and historical inheritance of sin' are restored to themselves and are not to be exploited as an object of men's desire. In this way they experience love 'which finds direct expression in Christ'. This is the liberation that faith brings. Women are freed in their relationship to Christ by their relationship with Christ and in so doing they find the true meaning of being a woman. 'christology does not exclude or suppress the female aspect as inconsequential, and that recognition of the female role does not diminish christology, says Joseph Ratzinger, 'only in the right co-ordination of one to the other can we discover the truth about God and ourselves.'[65] Mary, the mother of Jesus, emerges as the model of this liberation in action. Ratzinger has observed that Mary's song does not codify her dependency or glorify women's oppression. On the other hand it does not advocate the overthrow of established social structure. *Mulieris dignitatem* points out that the freedom of the *Magnificat* for women is in the restoration of their true femininity as designed by God and proclaimed by Jesus, 'for in appearing and acting in this way, [he] made it clear that the mysteries of the kingdom were known to him in every detail'.

Following Mary's example, many women from the church's history are held up as instances of women's true feminine dignity being honoured and promoted. These women, the pope argues, have been able to achieve liberation, restoration, love of Christ and transformation of the world in the church 'from one generation to the next ... Even in the face of serious social discrimination, holy women have acted freely, strengthened in their union with Christ.'

Mary and Martha

In the light of this understanding of the church's contribution to women's liberation, *Mulieris dignitatem* takes two accounts of scripture to focus on the type of liberation Jesus actually enabled women to achieve in their own world. Having made the point that the woman at the well (John 4:27-42) was transformed from being a sinful woman to being a disciple, *Mulieris dignitatem* goes on to point out that such an event was unprecedented in Israel, 'whereas in Jesus of Nazareth's way of acting, such an event becomes normal'. The document looks at Mary in Luke 10:38-42, and Martha in John 11:21-27 as further demonstrations of this activity.

Mary of Bethany, *Mulieris dignitatem* reiterates, listened to the

---

65. Ratzinger, J., 'The signs of the woman', in H. von Balthasarr, Mary: God's Yes to Man, San Francisco: Ignatius Press, 1987, p. 19.

teaching of Jesus in spite of the remonstrations of Martha (Luke 10:40) for her to help with the household duties. Mary is rewarded for choosing the better part, while Martha is admonished for being preoccupied with domestic matters.

As we have seen in the earlier work on papal use of scripture, this story is interpreted not in isolation, but as part of the whole of scripture. To that end, as Ratzinger states, 'a historico-critical exegesis is presupposed'.[66] *Mulieris dignitatem* then implicitly demonstrates an understanding of the historical situation behind the text.

The document seems to operate out of the following presumptions about the text: the focus of Luke 10:38-42 is not only on Mary listening to Jesus' teaching, but more precisely on the position Mary assumes. 'Mary, who sat at the Lord's feet, listened to what he was saying' [NRSV]. The force of the text is in the pose of a student learning from the master. The picture is that of a rabbi instructing his pupil. The extraordinary feature is that the pupil is a woman. Further still, the text seems to presume that the pose Mary has adopted is not just for the one occasion but that the relationship between Jesus as teacher and a woman as student is something for the future. 'Mary has chosen the better path which will not be taken away from her' [NRSV]. This is unheard of in Rabbinic Judaism. 'Jewish women, in this tradition, were not permitted to be taught the Torah, but only instructed about how they should live their lives in obedience to its commands. They were not permitted to touch the scriptures or to take part in public debate or official liturgical ritual.'[67] This is the 'concrete and historical situation of women' which Jesus

---

66. ibid., p. 11.

67. See J. Fitzmyer, *The Gospel according to St Luke*, New York: Doubleday, 1985, p. 892; W. Swidler, *Women in Judaism: The Status of Women in Formative Judaism*, Metuchen, NJ: The Scarecrow Press, 1976, chap.4; A. Brenner, *The Israelite Woman: Social Role and Literary Type in Biblical Narrative*, Sheffield: JSOT Press, 1985, chap. 8.

entered and, in allowing Mary to assume the characteristic of a student, liberated her from it.

Mulieris dignitatem concludes that this liberation, when viewed through the whole message of Christ to women, reveals that the most profound mysteries of God are to be shared with women and they are to be encouraged to respond as fully as Mary of Bethany with 'true resonance of mind and heart, a response of faith'.

Martha of Bethany, in John 11:21-27, is said in *Mulieris dignitatem* to have one of the most important conversations in the gospels. To Martha is revealed the 'most profound truths of revelation and faith ... "I am the resurrection and the life; those who believe in me, even though they die, will live and everyone who lives and believes in me will never die. Do you believe this?" "Yes, Lord; I believe that you are the Messiah, the Son of God, the one coming into the world" [NRSV]' (par. 15).

The document recognizes the importance of Jesus' love for Martha and Mary in the Gospel of John (John 11:5). As Raymond Brown observes, this comment is not without consequence. For in this gospel the central figure is the disciple whom Jesus loved. 'The only other people to receive that description from the writer of John is Martha and her sister [Mary] and Lazarus.' This love of Jesus is intimately linked to discipleship. 'Discipleship is the primary Christian category for John, and the disciple par excellence is the disciple whom Jesus loved ... And so it is noteworthy that John would report that Jesus loved Martha and Mary.'[68]

It is this extraordinary role Martha has in the fourth gospel that *Mulieris dignitatem* highlights as a model of the liberation Jesus brings all women. However this liberation to be a disciple is quite specific in the document: it is the ability of women to respond out of their

---

68. Brown, R., 'Roles of women in the fourth gospel', *Theological Studies*, 316 (1975), p. 694.

distinctly feminine disposition that enables them to become 'an incarnation of the feminine ideal ... a model for all Christians, a model of the *sequela Christi*.'

In terms of the liberation Jesus offers women, *Mulieris dignitatem* is a good example of how papal teaching understands the liberating activity of Christ as an apostolic mission for the church. This mission has been fulfilled over the centuries. It is based on Jesus' own words and actions in the gospels, particularly in Luke 10 and John 11, the stories of Mary and Martha. These, when read against the background of the church's tradition, emphasize that the freedom Jesus gives women through the church is to have the mysteries of God revealed to them (Mary) and then confess faith in Christ (Martha) through 'the feminine response in mind and heart'.

Fiorenza on Martha and Mary

Elizabeth Schüssler Fiorenza has written about Martha and Mary extensively.69 Her interests have concentrated much more on the Lucan narrative than on John 11; however, she does see in these two events an important basis from which to look at the implications for women's relationship with Jesus.

That Jesus brings women liberation is a crucial part of her theological framework, but the liberation Jesus offers to women is social, religious and political. Consequently, Fiorenza reads the two texts under consideration in the light of her political agenda. 'A feminist biblical interpretation is thus first of all a political task. It remains

69. Fiorenza, E. S., 'A feminist critical interpretation for liberation: Martha and Mary: Luke 10:38-42', *Religion and Intellectual Life*, 3 (1986), pp. 21-35; Fiorenza, E. S., *In Memory of Her*, pp. 165ff & 329ff; Fiorenza, E. S., 'Theological criteria and historical reconstruction: Martha and Mary in Luke 10:38-42', *Protocol of the Centre for Hermeneutical Studies*, 53, 1986, pp. 1-12.

mandatory because the Bible and its authority has been and is again today used as a weapon against women struggling for liberation.'[70]

Given that this starting point is clearly and openly stated, Fiorenza applies her four-fold hermeneutic. We will examine how this is applied first to Luke 10:35-42 and then to John 11:1-46.

Fiorenza begins her critical study by disclaiming that Luke 10:35ff is a feminist liberating text just because the central characters are women. By applying a hermeneutic of suspicion, Fiorenza assumes that the text is basically androcentric and should be initially read as a support and defence of patriarchal power. Fiorenza concludes that, approached with this suspicion, Luke 10:38ff. can be seen as a story that has often been used within a 'good women/bad women polarization'.

This is evidenced by three traditional interpretations of this story. The first is that it gives women a choice between the active life and the contemplative life. Active women (Martha) serve the needs of husbands and children, while passive women (Mary) serve the needs of Christ, their bridegroom; The second is that women should provide for the material needs of others in the Christian community (Martha), but should also take time to pray (Mary). The one duty should complement the other privilege. The third is that Mary vindicates women who wish to study theology and proves that Jesus rejects traditional Rabbinic Jewish roles of housewife as women's only choice. While a variety of other interpretations have been forwarded over the centuries, Fiorenza concludes that the text reinforces, one way or another, 'the dualistic antagonism between the two women or between the timeless principles of lifestyles the women symbolize'.

Fiorenza rejects this dualistic interpretation as androcentric, and

---

70. Fiorenza, E. S., 'Continuing our critical work', p. 129.

in her hermeneutic of remembrance moves to establish what the situation of the community was that would lead to such a story.

Owing to the fact that in this Lucan text *Kyrios* (Lord) is used, that women are in such a prominent role and that the action of the story revolves around the issue of *diakonia* (service) in a house setting, Fiorenza argues that the situation is commentating on the life of the Lucan community. More precisely it is addressing the conflict that has arisen in the community as a result of the leadership of women. Martha's *diakonia* is of central concern here, for *diakonia* in Luke's time had already become a technical term for ecclesial leadership. So while Mary is approved for being silent at the feet of the Lord, Martha who is active, mobile, possibly missionary, is silenced. Fiorenza concludes that the 'text is not descriptive of an actual situation, but it is prescriptive.' Women's ministry and authority, which seem to have been a prominent part of the Lucan community, are challenged. The text's 'rhetorical interests [are] to silence women leaders of house churches who, like Martha, might have protested, and, at the same time, to extol the silent and subordinate behaviour of Mary.'

The hermeneutic of proclamation follows. Fiorenza argues that the analysis undertaken in critically remembering the ministry of the women in the Lucan community raises the theological question of whether this story and others like it should remain in the canon of scripture. Given that, at its root, it outlines the gradual patriarchalization of the church in the first century, Fiorenza argues for a canon within a canon which would see this narrative relegated to the outer canon. 'We do not accord to such a patriarchal text divine authority and proclaim it as the Word of God. Instead we must proclaim it as the word of Luke!' In doing this, women today reclaim for themselves the memory of their foresisters who were alienated and oppressed, and in their name continue to fight for the liberation Jesus brought them and offers now.

Finally, then, Fiorenza's hermeneutic of actualization and ritualization starts with remembering the Martha and Mary tradition in
Luke, but in the light of women's experience.[71] This means that many
women identify with Martha being active and outspoken and resent
the traditional silent feminine role Mary portrays. Consequently, the
text needs to be re-interpreted with historical imagination, artistry
and liturgical sensibility. In this way the story is retold, rediscov-
ered for 'our own struggles against patriarchal subordination, silenc-
ing and oppression as one and the same struggle for liberation and
wholeness.'

Turning to John 11:1-46, Fiorenza, of course, initially assumes
that the text actively works to marginalize women and to play
down their role in the narrative. Certainly, it is true that Mary and
Martha have often been seen to be somewhat hysterical in their grief
for Lazarus, thereby reinforcing a gender specific stereotype. However, Fiorenza concludes that the entire synoptic tradition and more
especially John's gospel show that Mary and Martha were 'well-
known apostolic figures in the early church ... They are [Jesus'] true
disciples and he is their teacher.'

The hermeneutic of remembrance, when applied to John 11,
enables the reader to see the importance of Mary and Martha in the
life of the early church. As was observed with *Mulieris dignitatem's*
reading of the text, Martha's confession of faith parallels Peter's,
especially in Matthew 16:15-19. 'Thus Martha represents the full
apostolic faith of the Johannine community just as Peter does for
the Matthean community.'[72] Fiorenza, however, takes the analysis
another step by including chapter 12:1-8 in the narrative as well,
thereby giving Mary the central role in the ministry of service. So,

---

71. Fiorenza, E. S., Theological criteria and historical reconstruction', p. 4.
72. Fiorenza, E. S., 'A feminist critical interpretation for liberation: Martha and
    Mary: Luke 10:38-42', p. 31.

'while Martha of Bethany is responsible for the articulation of the community's christological faith, Mary of Bethany exemplifies the right praxis of discipleship'. Both of these elements are critical to the overall theological aim of the gospel. As Brown has observed, 'the evangelist is writing in the 90s when the office of diakonos already existed in the post-Pauline churches to which the community or its leaders appointed individuals by laying on hands (Acts 6:1-6). In the Johannine community a woman could be described as exercising a function which in other churches was the function of an ordained person.'[73]

Fiorenza argues that the reality behind the text is, in a way, similar to that of Luke 10, namely that it reflects the struggle of early Christian women to have their ministry of word and service recognized by the patriarchal leaders of the time. Unlike Luke, the writer of John's gospel does not pit the two sisters against each other, but has them complement each other. In this way the 'fourth gospel indicates how women might have appealed to the leadership of women in the Jesus movement in order to legitimate their own ministry and authority' at the turn of the first century.

Although Fiorenza does not say it, one assumes that the hermeneutic of proclamation would leave this text in the internal canon for preaching and worship. This would occur first because it seems to be a biblical story which does not reflect the reinforcement of patriarchal power, but conversely works to articulate a theology of inclusion, complementarity and vindication of women's ministry. In fact, Fiorenza may conclude that John 11-12:8 portrays not just the leadership and presence of women but 'the visible tip of an iceberg which for the most part is submerged'.

To this end, proclamation of this text will enable contempo-

---

73. Brown, R., 'Roles of women in the fourth gospel', pp. 690-691.

rary women to reclaim Mary and Martha as models of the ordained women ministers of the Johannine tradition. It certainly reinforces a dynamic understanding of, and legitimation for, the liberation of women into roles of leadership in word and service in Christ's name.

Finally, Fiorenza's hermeneutic of actualization and ritualization means that John 11-12:8 becomes the basis for feminist liturgy, imagination and creativity. 'We create feminist rituals for celebrating our foremothers ... sing litanies of praise to our foresisters and pray laments for the wasted lives of our foremothers.' To this end Fiorenza maintains that Martha and Mary model the liberation Jesus brings all women by drawing out their role as ordained ministers, disciple-leaders, and heralds of right theological words and actions.

Conclusions on liberation

Both John Paul II and Fiorenza agree that liberation comes to women in terms of a call to discipleship. The pope, however, defines discipleship within the terms of gender distinctions. True to his letter's traditional belief that God has created differences to effect different ends, the document argues that women's liberation most appropriately occurs in terms of their gender specific position in society. Put simply this means that women are freed to be women by Jesus. Women are invited to full intimate union with Jesus and as women are called to witness to him in the world. The most appropriate response women can make to this invitation and call, the document argues, is for them to develop their essential feminine originality and richness. In this way they become for the world the feminine image and likeness of the Creator, in the way the Creator intended them to be.

On the other hand, Fiorenza, in working out of her social and political agenda, argues that Jesus brings to women a liberation from patriarchy and an equal call to discipleship with men. This should be manifest in their ordination to the ministry of word and sacrament. Fiorenza holds that from her standpoint it seems impossible that the 'Vatican has appealed to the authority of Christ, the apostles, and tradition in order to legitimate patriarchal church structures that exclude women from sacramental, doctrinal and governing power on the basis of sex'.[74] As we have seen, Fiorenza in her hermeneutic reclaims the same sources as 'the Vatican' to argue that women are called to equal status and service in the church: 'We have called for the conversion of the whole church to the discipleship community of equals which Jesus initiated, the apostolic churches continued and Vatican II reaffirmed'.[75]

The mission Jesus gives women: apostle to the Apostles

Mary Magdalene is for John Paul an outstanding example of the vocation all women receive from Jesus. In John 20:1-18, the evangelist narrates the interaction between Jesus and Mary Magdalene in the garden on Easter Sunday morning. Mary, as first witness to the Risen Christ, is 'also the first to bear witness to him before the Apostles'. It is this commission to witness to Christ that is remarkable. 'This event, in a sense, crowns all that has been said previously about Christ entrusting divine truths to women as well as men.'

Mulieris dignitatem brings to the biblical text a clear understanding of the social implications of Jesus' activity in John 20:1-18. Jesus should not have been talking to a woman in public and certainly the idea of sending a woman to inform men of a religious or personal phenomenon was not acceptable in the social or legal customs of

---

74. Fiorenza, E. S., 'The discipleship of equals', *Commonweal*, August 1985, p. 433.
75. ibid., p. 434.

first century Palestine. At very least, the narrative presents a breakthrough in the conduct of men toward women.

However the reality of the inauguration of a new liberty in male/female relationships is but one of the issues involved in this narrative. *Mulieris dignitatem* gives this particular focus such prominence in chapter nine because of the critical role Mary Magdalene's witness has assumed in contemporary interpretations. More will be said of this later when Fiorenza's exposition on John 20 is analyzed.

Given what has already been said at the beginning of this chapter regarding Jesus' charge to Peter and the apostles to proclaim the gospel as the mandate for papal authority, it is critical in *Mulieris dignitatem* that Jesus' charge to Mary Magdalene to witness be appropriately understood. The issue here is not merely one of semantics, for she has been interpreted through history as anything from a hysterical woman grieving over her lover's death to the first and most important Christian apostle and evangelist. The issue that evolves, then, is that Mary Magdalene's commission can be seen to threaten the primacy of Peter's charge, and so the very centre of papal hermeneutics is challenged.

Mulieris dignitatem is not intent on playing down the role of Mary, but seeing it in the context of the mission given to the entire Christian community. In fact the document states that within several of the resurrection narratives Mary Magdalene has a special role. This is especially true in John. However, as Hans von Balthasar writes, 'In the New Testament ... there is one single total truth, one single dogma, which at its centre is christological ... as well as soteriological'.[76]

In this light the document assesses the role and interpretation of Magdalene's witness in terms of Jesus' relationship to all women and

---

76. Von Balthasar H., *Convergences*, San Francisco: Ignatius Press, 1969, p. 93.

all members of the church. Hence *Mulieris dignitatem* does not engage in any attempt to look at precisely what John 20 means but accepts this passage within 'the larger biblical unity ... [as a] testimony about true relationships between God and us'.

Granted these principles, *Mulieris dignitatem* accepts the prominent role of Mary Magdalene as a witness to the resurrection, that 'unique act by which God transformed and raised for ever the person Jesus to his right hand'.[77] The people who had this experience were given significant honour. Proof of such an experience was required to validate apostolic authority.[78]

A witness to the resurrection, says Gerald O'Collins, either had to have had an apparition of the risen Lord or discovered the empty tomb. Mary Magdalene, in the Synoptic tradition, has the latter, while in John's gospel she experiences both.

Mulieris dignitatem turns to Christian tradition to help assess the appropriate understanding Magdalene should have for women today.[79] Consequently, it invokes St Thomas Aquinas' title for Magdalene, 'the apostle to the Apostles'. The small case 'a' in apostle is critical here, as *Mulieris dignitatem* teaches that Mary does not claim to herself the same role or status as the Twelve.

On this point, *Mulieris dignitatem* is fully supported by the Pontifical Biblical Commission who, when asked to report on the biblical evidence regarding women being admitted to the priesthood, stated,

---

77. O'Collins, G. & Kendall D., 'Mary Magdalene as major witness to the resurrection', *Theological Studies*, 48 (1987), p. 634.

78. See Paul: 'I saw the Lord Jesus', 1 Corinthians 9:1-2; 15:8-11; Galatians 1:11-16.

79. By doing this, it can be observed how the magisterium understands the way in which tradition illuminates scripture. 'The church does not draw her certainty about all revealed truths from the holy Scriptures alone, but relies on sacred tradition and the living teaching office of the church for an authentic interpretation.' See *Dei Verbum* ('Constitution on Divine Revelation'), *Documents of Vatican II*, sections 9-10.

'Jesus, during his ministry chose a group of twelve men who after the fashion of twelve patriarchs of the Old Testament, would be leaders of the renewed people of God.'[80] The report outlines that although Mary Magdalene's role is emphasized and women like her are invited into a positive collaborative ministry in the Christian community, 'we can know [that] those who held a role of leadership in the communities ... were always men, in conformity with Jewish custom.'

So how is Magdalene's mission to be understood and appropriated? Magdalene's witness to the resurrection is seen in *Mulieris dignitatem* to be akin to prophecy. Just as women prophets announced the revelation of God to the people of Israel, so Magdalene proclaims the revelation of Christ's resurrection to the new Israel. She is the first instance of God's words being fulfilled: that your daughters will prophesy (Joel 3:1). This occurs as a result of the action of God's Spirit raising Jesus from the dead.

In this light, Magdalene is no threat to the primacy of Peter. For Peter remains, when the whole scripture is read in the light of the whole tradition, the spokesperson for the community of Jesus' disciples, the defender of Christ's commands, the first among equals within the apostolic community and the leader of post-Easter ministry. It is within this ministry that women, with Magdalene as especially prominent, are commissioned to witness, to prophesy.

So what of the contemporary implication of Magdalene's witness? *Mulieris dignitatem* argues that it is a proof that Jesus is given in truth to women and men equally. To that end, the Christian community is one of equality and this should be safeguarded and promoted. The church should be a place where women are enabled to 'receive his salvific and sanctifying visits'. In this way the church continues to remain faithful to the apostolic charge of being one, where being

---

80. Pontifical Biblical Commission, *Report on admission of women to the priesthood*, Rome, 1977, part 4, sect. 2.

a woman or man, slave or free, Jew or Greek, makes no difference, 'for you are all one in Christ Jesus' (Galatians 3:28).

However, 'this unity does not cancel out diversity'. Just as Mary Magdalene assumed no apostolic office but proclaimed what she had seen, so too women are called to do the same. And in this Magdalene was true to the originality of her womanhood: playing an active and important role in the life of the church in building it up from its foundation through her own gifts and talents. In this sense it could be said that Mary Magdalene preceded the many great women the document names from the tradition as models of the prophetic character of feminine love for Christ and the church. This is the vocation it advocates for all women in the world today.

First apostle to the Apostles

We have already seen in the preceding section that Elizabeth Schüssler Fiorenza maintains that Mary Magdalene is not only an apostle in every sense of the word, but that her apostolic role in the early church challenged the tradition which placed Peter as pre-eminent resurrection witness and leader.

Fiorenza reads John 20:1-18 suspicious that what is already occurring in the text is a playing down of Magdalene's role. While she recognizes that it is remarkable that Mary's primacy in being a witness to the resurrection has survived in two sources of gospel tradition, she asserts that the hand of a later editor can be seen in placing the beloved disciple, and even more so, Peter as the leading figures in the entire resurrection narratives.

Not only is the evidence for this claim from the text itself and other scholarly findings,[81] but also from the experiences of women

---

81. See R. Brown, *The Community of the Beloved Disciple*, New York, Paulist Press, 1979, pp. 30ff; R. Brown, 'Roles of women in the fourth gospel', pp. 183-98; S. Schneiders, 'Women in the fourth gospel and the role of women in the contemporary church', *Biblical Theology Bulletin*, 12 (1982), pp. 35-45.

and men today. Fiorenza states: 'When we think of Mary Magdalene, we do not think of her first as a Christian apostle and evangelist, rather we have before our eyes the image of Mary as the sinner and the penitent woman'.[82] Consequently, she concludes that the role of Magdalene has been edited in such a way as to attempt to 'limit women's leadership roles in the Christian community to be culturally and religiously acceptable'.[83] However, Fiorenza also believes that enough is present in the narratives of John and Mark to make it impossible for the Christian church to forget the apostolic and ministerial leadership women held in the Jesus movement and the early Christian communities.

The reconstruction of the world that lies behind these two gospel texts particularly and the person and role of Magdalene are of critical importance to Fiorenza. She sees in Mary Magdalene a paradigm of all women's experience in a patriarchal church and society and so the task of redressing the suppression of her memory as leader and founder takes on significant proportions. 'As women we should not have to reject the Christian faith and tradition, we have to reclaim women's contribution and role in it. We must free the images of Mary Magdalene from all distortions and recover her role as apostle.'[84]

Four issues emerge from Fiorenza's critical reading of the text that help establish a new understanding of its context and history. First, Magdalene is the perfect follower of Jesus, remaining faithful at the cross and now seeking to find him in the garden on Easter morning. She is the model of discipleship for the Johannine community, as they are exhorted to continue to seek for the Lord.

Second, Mary 'recognizes' the Lord and Jesus claims her as 'his

82. Fiorenza, E. S., 'Feminist theology as critical theology', p. 625.
83. Fiorenza, E. S., *In Memory of Her*, p. 334.
84. Fiorenza, E. S., 'Feminist theology as critical theology, p. 625.

own'. In this way Mary is pre-eminent as the Lord's own because she is first to see and hear Jesus after the resurrection.

Third, Magdalene is the primary witness to the resurrection and the first person to announce resurrection faith to the community. 'She was sent to the disciples to proclaim the Easter *Kerygma* ... Christian faith is based on the witness and proclamation of women.'[85] Although Mary's role in the events of the resurrection are most strongly attested to in the gospels of Mark and John, Fiorenza argues that the narratives of Matthew and Luke help establish women, and Mary Magdalene especially, as the first bearers of Jesus' new life to the community. 'According to all exegetical criteria of authenticity, this is an historical fact, for it could not have been derived from Judaism nor invented by the primitive church'.[86]

Finally, the history of women in the early church reveals that Magdalene, Martha, Salome, Phoebe and Mary of Bethany are appealed to in an attempt to demonstrate how women had been leaders of the Christian community from the beginning and therefore their ministry justifies women of subsequent generations enjoying the same role and status.

An important part of Fiorenza's reconstruction of Mary Magdalene's role is to look at the gnostic texts concerning her. For while the canonical gospels reduce the role and importance of women, 'the debate between patriarchal and egalitarian Christian groups is reflected in various gnostic texts which relate the competition between Peter and Mary Magdalene'.[87] Fiorenza accepts this literature for consideration because 'the texts that are included in the New Testament Canon only justify male leadership [and] record the sad demise of the original Christian vision of oneness in Christ.' To criti-

85. Fiorenza, E. S., 'Feminist theology as critical theology', p. 625.
86. ibid., p. 616.
87. Fiorenza E. S., 'Word, spirit and power', p. 52.

cally remember the world of Magdalene, a number of apocryphal documents are analyzed. Fiorenza argues that *The Great Questions of Mary*, *The Gospel of Thomas*, *Pistis Sophia* and *The Gospel of Mary Magdalene* reflect the prominence of Magdalene's leadership and outline how women's apostolic ministry came to be suppressed by men who claimed the superiority of Peter and the Petrine tradition.

Women today, then, should be empowered by Magdalene's commission. In their proclamation to the world, they should see Magdalene and the other women as 'paradigms of women's apostolic discipleship as their leadership in the Johannine community [testifies to]. As such they are not just paradigms of faithful discipleship to be imitated by women, but by all those who belong to Jesus' "very own familial community".'[88]

In this spirit, Fiorenza argues, women must go out to the church and world convinced that while the story of women's true vocation has all but been forgotten in the life of the church, the dangerous memory of Magdalene's leadership and service is kept alive.

Fiorenza encourages women to do this through her hermeneutic of actualization. She argues that all women should be apostles to the apostles. This means reclaiming Magdalene's role of authority, status and mission in the church. For just as Mary was 'sent to the disciples to proclaim the basic tenets of Christian faith so women today may rediscover by contemplating her image the important function and role they have for the Christian faith and community'.[89]

88. Fiorenza, E. S., *In Memory of Her*, p. 333.
89. Fiorenza, E. S., *Feminist theology as critical theology*, p. 625.

Chapter 8

Towards a Fruitful Dialogue

THE CONTRASTING METHODOLOGIES investigated above raise several questions. Here we will look briefly at three: How can scripture be read or the christological tradition be accepted in a way that meets the concerns of women in the church? Given the long and well-tested effectiveness of its hermeneutics, what responsibility does papal teaching have to revise its own hermeneutic? On the other hand, is there an ethic of accountability for both the feminist scholars and the pope in this dialogue? If so, what is it?

It is a most unusual occurrence for the Vatican to respond in a direct way to a school of theology or biblical criticism. The only recent example of a direct confrontation with a school of theology, other than to ask for clarification from its individual exponents,[90] was that with the liberation theologians of Latin America.[91]

However, the Pontifical Biblical Commission, a consultative body to the Congregation for the Doctrine of the Faith, refers to feminist hermeneutics in its most recent document on bibli-

---

90. Among theologians who have been asked for this clarification are Hans Küng, Leonardo Boff, Edward Schillebeeckx, Matthew Fox and Charles Curran.
91. Congregation for the Doctrine of the Faith, *Libertatis nuntius*, Rome, 6 August 1984.

114

cal interpretation.[92] It criticizes three approaches in the feminist school:

— those who reject the Bible as irretrievably androcentric;

— those who propose a feminist canon within the canon;

— those who seek to reclaim the lost history of women and the discipleship of equals.

Elizabeth Schüssler Fiorenza is the leading exponent of this final approach.

As a precursor to this statement, *Mulieris dignitatem* stands as an indirect response to several of the questions, challenges and conclusions of these schools and their dependent methodologies. For while it is a 'meditation' — a pastoral homily — given for the edification of women in the church and for the world at large, it is also an opportunity to redress the imbalance of the theological input the Vatican observes has occurred on the issue of women's rights in recent years. It states this in its opening paragraph: 'The dignity and the vocation of women — a subject of constant human and Christian [my emphasis] reflection — have gained exceptional pre-eminence in recent years.'

At the end, the document returns to this point: contemporary reflection on and changes to the thinking about women and women's role in church and society. It warns that the 'significant changes of our times' can only be correct and adequate if we follow the truth of Christ, mediated through the teaching office of the church. 'A different way of acting would lead to doubtful, if not actually erroneous and deceptive results.' And so it urges women again to meditate on the biblical mystery of 'the woman', Mary, mother of God, and discover through her their supreme vocation: motherhood and virginity.

---

92. See Pontifical Biblical Commission, *The Interpretation of the Bible in the Church*, Libreria Editrice Vaticana, 1993.

Mulieris dignitatem stands, then, as a rejection of a number of the conclusions – sociological, political, psychological and theological – that are emerging from the feminist theological schools internationally.

In light of this, any dialogue between the two has not been a direct exchange. It is much more an exchange of position to position. Hence, it is not possible to compare John Paul's position directly with that of Elizabeth Schüssler Fiorenza on the questions cited above. It is quite legitimate, however, to compare her thought on these issues to that of Cardinal Joseph Ratzinger. Though not speaking officially, that is, on behalf of the church in his position as Prefect of the Congregation for Doctrine of the Faith, he does represent the stance assumed in papal theological hermeneutics. Ratzinger illustrates intelligent, logical, Roman thought, and much of what he has to say of feminist hermeneutics addresses both the questions raised in this study and reflects the content and hermeneutic of *Mulieris dignitatem*.

How can scripture and tradition be seen as good news for women in the church today?

Well before the Pontifical Biblical Commission's document, Cardinal Joseph Ratzinger had been quite specific in his condemnation of the feminist biblical school's answer to this question. In an essay entitled, 'Biblical interpretation in crisis: on the question of the foundations and approaches of exegesis today'.[93] Ratzinger denounces exegesis that excludes supernatural explanations and renders theologically 'barren analyses of sources.' He offers two examples of this type of exegesis, materialist and feminist exegesis. These approaches, he maintains, seek to recon-

---

93. See J. Ratzinger, 'Biblical interpretation in crisis: on the foundations and approaches of exegesis today', in R. J. Neuhams (ed.), *Biblical Interpretation in Crisis*, Grand Rapids, Mich: Eerdmans, 1989, pp. 1-24.

struct the text based on suspicion rather than what is actually in the text. This reference is a direct rebuttal of the Fiorenza methodology.

Ratzinger also believes that this hermeneutic of suspicion is leading women and men astray and states that its attendant exegeses are not taken seriously by other scholars: '... the radical hermeneutics I have just described have already been disavowed by a large number of exegetes'. He believes that the historical reconstructionist model of theological and biblical interpretation which Fiorenza works out of, 'leads to the sprouting of ever more numerous hypotheses which finally turn into a jungle of contradictions'.

The central problem, Ratzinger observes, is in the way feminist exegesis does not attempt to understand the text in terms of what was originally intended. Rather, 'one no longer learns what the text says, but what it should have said, and by which component parts this can be traced back through the text'. This situation arises because feminist biblical scholars and theologians are driven by their plan for social, political or religious reform, and therefore the text and its meaning are distorted. 'In this sense, they are no longer interested in ascertaining the truth, but only in whatever will serve their own particular agendas.'

Ratzinger has no problem with tracing back texts to their original historical setting and looking at them in context; in fact he encourages this. But the reading of these observations and inquiries must happen 'in the light of the total movement of history and in light of history's central event, Jesus Christ'.

Further, interpretation must happen in sympathia with the historical faith of the Christian assembly. In this way the theologian and exegete comes to 'a readiness to learn something new, to allow oneself to be taken along a new road'. This sympathia, Ratzinger argues, avoids subjecting the text to 'just any kind of enthusiasm', which 'dissects the Bible into discontinuous pieces, which are then able to be put to new use and inserted into a new montage altogether different from the original biblical context'.

Can the teaching office of the church revise its own hermeneutic in a way that addresses the concerns of women, and yet is true to tradition? Ratzinger concludes that theological enquiry and biblical criticism do not take place in a vacuum, but occur as a result of the life of the church. He denounces scholarly schools that approach the scripture or tradition out of their particular philosophy or scientific world-views, and consequently read them from these positions. He maintains that this approach 'determines in advance what may or may not be'.

This is not acceptable. The exegete and theologian must read scripture inside the church, inside Christian faith for 'without faith the Bible remains a closed book ... [and] history is the proper space for the process of coming to understand the text.' In saying this, Ratzinger also rejects 'a merely positivistic and rigid ecclesiasticism which selects the findings of exegesis which support the dogmatic or traditional teaching of the church'. What he does believe is that the task of theology and biblical scholarship belongs to the living experience of the church expressed in its liturgy. Here the criteria for exegesis and orthodoxy are established. In this light, 'the last word belongs to the church, but the church must also give the last word to the Bible.'

Is there an ethical base to scriptural and dogmatic interpretation? Elizabeth Schüssler Fiorenza does in part answer some of Cardinal Ratzinger's questions and challenges in writing about the ethics of hermeneutics. Fiorenza would claim that Ratzinger's and her understanding of the exegete's task are so divergent because their starting points are different. Far from her seeing her work for women's liberation from patriarchy as 'just any kind of enthusiasm', which distorts her reading of scripture and tradition, she sees it as a service to the church, a task of continuing the liberating praxis of Jesus and the movement he founded.

Fiorenza could see Ratzinger's approach as unethical. Once biblical scholarship begins to 'talk explicitly of social interests, whether of race, gender, culture or class and once it begins to recognize the need for a sophisticated and pluralistic reading of texts that questions the fixity of meaning, then a double ethics is called for'.[94]

This double ethics involves, first, an ethics of historical reading which looks to what people, interests and world-views are being promoted and imposed over the interests of others in the text itself. It takes seriously the political and social nature and intention of texts and their authors.

Second, an ethics of accountability takes responsibility for not only what the text says but how the tradition has used these texts to promote dehumanization. Fiorenza names anti-Semitism, misogyny, slavery and war as just a few examples of the abuse of the scriptural record supported by the church over history.

Fiorenza, as we have seen, believes that the Bible and the Christian tradition are basically androcentric. Consequently, she advocates interpreting all texts in the church's history through rhetorical criticism, asking, 'How is meaning constructed? Whose interests are served? What kind of worlds are envisioned? What roles, duties and values are advocated? Which social-political practices are legitimated?'

For her the task of an exegete or theologian is not to pretend that they are detached, objective and value-neutral, nor to feel as if they are bound by dogmatic or ecclesiastical control, but that their work, their interpretation of that work and its application 'could

---

94. Fiorenza, E. S., 'The ethics of biblical interpretation', in *The Journal of Biblical Literature*, 107, 1988, p. 14.

be a significant participant in the global discourse seeking justice and well being for all'. Fiorenza sees this task at the heart of Jesus' mission to the church.

Conclusion

Finding a Middle Ground

THERE ARE MANY POSITIVE aspects to papal teaching on women. It clearly contributes important insights and reflections to the discussion of women's dignity and vocation. Not only does this body of teaching address doctrinal questions, but it also confronts pastoral concerns. As a result, it carries within it the tensions of the pastoral life of the church as well. Having affirmed both the intrinsic equality of women as God's image and likeness and their rights to full personhood, it does not know how to reconcile that affirmation with women's vocation in the church.

Most readers of the two recent papal documents about women can basically agree with their endorsement of women's unquestionable dignity and equality to men. So the point of divergence is not the question of dignity. The central implication of the divergent approaches of the parties involved in the debate concerns women's vocation. This, in my opinion, is the tension which underpins the entire dialogue between women and papal teaching on women. Why?

First, no papal teaching or Vatican document concedes at any stage that the church has been instrumental in maintaining a history of discrimination against women. In fact, the documents seem proud of the tradition of the church in relation to women from the New Testament to the present day. However, what is striking about the

New Testament women they name (for example, 'Phoebe, a deacon of the church', Romans 16:11) is that in some cases their office in the church no longer exists; and some of the most important women are not mentioned at all.[95] Also, when *Mulieris dignitatem*, for example, mentions the women of the tradition who 'have shared in the church's mission' one of the common links between several of them is the confrontation they waged against male ecclesiastical authority or abuse in their day. This is certainly true for Birgitta of Sweden, Joan of Arc, Elizabeth Ann Seton, Mary Ward, Catherine of Siena and Teresa of Jesus.

Papal teaching would have been a richer and more comprehensive contribution to the discussion of women's vocation if it had been more self-critical. In an endeavour to promote women's vocation in contemporary society, it is necessary to recognize the activity of sin in the church's tradition and history towards women. It is also necessary to be open to the movement of conversion in attitude and activity in regard to women's vocation and call.

Second, John Paul II returns to the papal teaching of the 1950s to highlight Mary as a model for all women. This revision is not helpful. By not following on in the teaching line of John XXIII and Paul VI, John Paul displaces the relationship women have directly with Jesus. Through baptism, Galatians says, we are all one in Christ. It is in and through Christ that all Christians find their human identity – male or female. It is in Christ and in relation to Christ that Mary found her dignity and vocation. This was the point of departure of the 1960s and 1970s that was so helpful. To return to Mary now, as the model for women, raises unnecessary questions

---

95. Leaders of the house communities: Mary (Acts 12:12); Apphia (Philemon:2); Lydia (Acts 16:14); Nympha (Colossians 4:15); and Chole (1 Corinthians 1:11). Quite strikingly, while *Mulieris dignitatem* draws heavily on the women mentioned in Romans 16, the only one it excludes is Junia (16:7), whom Paul calls 'first among the apostles'.

christologically. For just as in Christ we all have our being, so in Mary we all – women and men – find a model of being in Christ. Christ is for all and Mary is for all. One is the mirror and the other is an exemplary reflection.

Associated with this revision is Mary's promotion as virgin and mother which is not helpful in an age that has seen women emerge strongly in social, political and professional leadership. Leaving aside the question of women's ordination to the priesthood, the modelling of women's options in terms of virginity and motherhood undermines a more hopeful reading of the Holy Spirit's action in the signs of the times. Again, John XXIII and Paul VI drew attention to this and encouraged women to be reach their full potential in society. Women's leadership in the world since 1978, in a cross-section of areas, has been outstanding. John Paul II could have recognized this and encouraged it.

Third, on a more linguistic level the entire language of all the documents, both in Latin and English, is exclusive. It never uses anything but the masculine pronoun to describe God, though *Mulieris dignitatem* states that feminine images ascribed to God are appropriate and this reflects how our language tries to capture the otherness of God. It constantly refers to humanity – women and men – as 'man', which is now seriously criticized by governments, universities, publishing houses and the media as being discriminatory towards women.

This concern is also connected with the issue of women's vocation, in that, when women are subsumed into man, in a generic sense, they do not emerge in their own right, as their own persons. Language reflects the presumptions of the writer, for better or worse. In the case of papal teaching, women are held as exemplars of the human genius but are constantly called 'man'.

All this being said, papal documents about women must be taken on their own terms. They have a particular hermeneutic that sets the terms clearly for argumentation and response. To understand these documents, one must enter their world and not criticize them for not being like some other statement from some other group. We have tried to highlight this difference of approach by contrasting Mulieris dignitatem with the hermeneutic of a leading influential feminist school. In doing so, we have demonstrated that *Mulieris dignitatem* is an important work, not so much in what it says, but more in clarifying the position and approach of the teaching/institutional church in the dialogue.

What is most clear is that this dialogue must continue. The divergent starting points operative in each participant's hermeneutic, must be addressed. If they are not, then not only is the dialogue in danger, but so is the church. The difficulty of Cardinal Ratzinger's approach, as reflected in papal teaching, is that the tradition and experience of the church is the appropriate place to interpret and define women's vocation. Yet, a growing number of faithful women (and men) are feeling alienated from that very same tradition and the current life of the church. They cannot see, in these documents, a reflection of their own vocation, as consonant with their own faith and talents, or a witness to the liberation and mission Jesus gave women.

While the argument can be understood in terms of an idealized versus an ideological reading of history, both extremes in this debate need to recognize the respective polarization operative in their methodology. There is middle ground, and it can be found.

The negative responses to John Paul II's *Ordinatio sacerdotalis* confirm that the question of women's dignity and vocation is of such moment for Catholicism that if ignored then, at best, an unofficial or underground church will develop, or, at worst, schism may occur. Worse still, women may quietly withdraw friom the church and discourage their children from any involvement with it.

The popes, throughout these documents, repeatedly address women as their 'beloved daughters'. Papal teaching has splendidly underlined the dignity of all human beings as sisters and brothers. The recognition of that dignity calls for forms of church teaching in which it is clear that brothers are listening to their sisters as well as fatfers are teaching their daughters.

A Select Bibliography

Baum, G., 'Bulletin: The Apostolic letter *Mulieris dignitatem*', *Concilium*, vol. 206 (1990), pp. 144-149.

—— 'The church and the women's movement', *The Ecumenist*, November-December 1988, pp. 12-15.

Bownan, J., *The Fourth Gospel and the Jews*, Pittsburgh: Pickwick, 1975.

Brenner, A., *The Israelite Woman: Social Role and Literary Type in Biblical Narrative*, Sheffield: JSOT Press, 1985.

Brown, R., *The Gospel according to John*, New York: Doubleday, vol. 1, 1970.

—— 'Roles of women in the fourth gospel', *Theological Studies*, 36 (1975), pp. 688-699.

Byrne, B., 'The faith of the beloved disciple and the community of John 20', *Journal for the Study of the New Testament*, 23 (1985), pp. 83-97.

—— Paul and the Christian Woman, Homebush: St Paul Publications, 1988.

Cahill, L. S., 'Sex and gender', *America*, vol. 162, no. 8 (1990), pp. 197-200.

—— 'Feminist Ethics', *Theological Studies*, 51 (1990), pp. 49-64.

Camp, R., *The Papal Ideology of Social Reform*, Leiden: Brill, 1969.

Carr, A., *Transforming Grace*, San Francisco: Harper & Row, 1988.

Carr, A., & Fiorenza, E. S. (eds), 'Editorial', *Concilium*, vol. 206, 1989, pp. 6-11.

Commission for the Role of Women in the Church and Society, 'Recommendations', *L'Osservatore Romano*, 12 August 1976. pp. 4-5.

Congregation for the Doctrine of the Faith, 'Declaration on certain questions regarding the admission of women to the ministerial priesthood', Rome, 1976.

Coste, R., 'La lettre apostolique *Mulieris dignitatem* de Jean Paul II sur la dignité et la vocation de la femme', *Espirit et Vie*, 45 (1988), pp. 610-624.

Daly, M., *The Gospel according to Women: Christianity's Creation of the Sex War in the West*, New York: Anchor Press, 1987.

—— *Beyond God the Father*, Boston: Beacon Press, 1973.

—— *Gyn-Ecology*, Boston: Beacon Press, 1978.

Doheny, W., & Kelly, J. P., *Papal Documents on Mary*, Milwaukee: Bruce Publishing, 1954.

Dorr, D., *Option for the Poor: A Hundred Years of Vatican Social Teaching*, Maryknoll, NY: Orbis, 1983.

Evans, M., *Woman in the Bible*, Exeter: Paternoster Press, 1973.

Fiorenza, Elisabeth Schüssler, *Bread not Stone*, Boston: Beacon Press, 1985.

A Select Bibiography

—— 'Philosophy of feminist biblical hermeneutics', unpublished conference paper, presented at 'Toward a Feminist Theology', Sydney, August 1989.

—— 'Feminist theology as a critical theology of liberation' *Theological Studies*, (36) 1975 p.624-629.

—— 'The politics of otherness: biblical interpretation as a critical praxis for liberation', in *The Future of Liberation Theology*, M. Ellis & O. Maduro (eds), Maryknoll, NY: Orbis, 1989.

—— *In Memory of Her*, New York: Crossroad, 1983.

Flannery, A., *Documents of Vatican II*, New York: Costello, 1975.

Gebara, J., 'The mother superior and spiritual motherhood: from intuition to institution', *Concilium*, vol. 206, 1990, pp. 42-51.

Gebara, J., & Bingemer J., *Mary Mother of God Mother of the Poor*, Maryknoll, NY: Orbis, 1989.

Giraldo, J. S. B., 'Communion y partecipacion: Presupusestos para una nueva imagen de familia', *Studia Moralia*, 27 (1989), pp. 159-176.

Glendon, M. A., 'A greater attention to women's dignity', *L'Osservatore Romano*, 45, 7 November 1988, p. 5.

Gomas F., 'Christology and pastoral practice from below', *East Asian Pastoral Review*, vol. 1 (1982).

Grassi, J., *The Hidden Heroes of the Gospels*, Collegeville, MN: Liturgical Press, 1989.

Greer, G., 'A more profound understanding of the feminine "person" and the plan of salvation', *L'Osservatore Romano*, 45, 7 November 1988, p. 5.

Hardesty, N., & Scanzani L., *All We're Meant To Be: A Biblical Approach to Women's Liberation*, Waco, Texas: Word Books, 1974.

Hebblethwaite, M., 'Pope seems more conservative than misogynist', *National Catholic Reporter*, 25, 11 November 1988, p. 15.

Heine, S., *Christianity and the Goddess*, London: SCM Press, 1988.

—— *Women and Earliest Christianity*, London: SCM Press, 1987.

Henriot, P., DeBerri P., Schultheis, M., *Catholic Social Teaching: Our Best Kept Secret*, Maryknoll, N.Y.: Orbis, 1988.

Hogan, A., 'The development of catholic social teaching since Leo XIII', *Compass*, 23, 1989.

Hunt, G., 'The Pope on the human vocation', *America*, 159, no. 11, 22 October 1988.

John Paul II, *Redemptoris Mater*, papal encyclical, Rome, 25 March 1987.

—— *Mulieris dignitatem*, apostolic letter, Rome, 15 August 1988.

—— *Laborem excercens*, papal encyclical, Rome, 14 September 1981.

—— *Familiaris consortio*, papal encyclical, Rome, 22 November 1981.

John XXIII, *Mater et magistra*, papal encyclical, Rome, 15 May 1961.

—— *Pacem in Terris*, papal encyclical, Rome, 11 April 1963.

Johnson, E., 'Jesus, the wisdom of God', *Ephemerides Theologiae Lovanianes*, 61 (1985), pp. 261-294.

—— *Consider Jesus: Waves of Renewal in Christology*, London: Chapman, 1990.

—— 'Christology's impact on the Doctrine of God', *Heythrop Journal*, xxvi (1985), pp. 158-170.

Johnson E. 'Reconstructing a Theology of Mary', in Mary, *Woman of Nazareth*, D. Donnelly(ed.), New York: Paulist Press, 1989.

King, V., 'The divine as mother', *Concilium*, 206, 1990, pp. 128-137.

Kohn-Roelin, J., 'Mother-daughter-God', *Concilium*, 206, 1990, pp. 64-72.

Lane, D., 'The incarnation of God in Jesus Christ', *Irish Theological Quarterly*, 46 (1979).

Latham, J., 'Male and female He created them, not masculine and feminine', *The Month*, 22 (1989), pp. 384-387.

Leo XIII, *Rerum novarum*, papal encyclical, Rome, 1891.

—— *Magnae Dei matris*, papal encyclical, Rome, 1892.

Maeckelberghe, E., 'Mary: maternal friend or virgin mother?', *Concilium*, 206 (1990), pp. 120-127.

McFague, S., 'Mother God', *Concilium*, 206 (1990), pp. 138-143.

—— *Metaphorical Theology*, London: SCM Press, 1983.

McGuire, M., *Religion: The Social Context*, Belmont, CA: Wadsworth, 1981.

McLaughlin, E., & Ruether, R. (eds), *Women of Spirit*, New York: Simon & Schuster, 1979.

Moloney F., 'John 20: a journey completed', *Australasian Catholic Record*, 59 (1982), pp. 420-430.

Moloney F., *Woman: First among the Faithful*, Melbourne: Dove Communications, 1984.

Moltmann-Wendel, E., 'Martha', in *The Women around Jesus*, London: SCM Press, 1982, pp. 15-22.

Monks of Solesmes, *The Woman in the Modern World*, Boston: St Paul, 1959.

O'Laoghaire, D., 'The dignity of women', *Doctrine and Life*, 39, February 1989, pp. 72-79.

Osiek, C., *Beyond Anger: On Being a Feminist in the Church*, New York: Paulist Press, 1986.

Paul VI, *Octogesima adveniens*, apostolic letter, Rome, 1971.

—— *Marialis cultus*, papal encyclical: Rome, 2 February 1974.

—— *Populorum progressio*, papal encyclical, Rome, 1967.

Pfafflin, U., 'Mothers in a patriarchal world: experience and feminist theory', *Concilium*, 206 (1990), pp. 15-22.

Pius X, *Ad diem illum*, papal encyclical, Rome, 1904.

Pius XI, *Casti connubi*, papal encyclical, Rome, 31 December 1930.

—— *Quadragesimo anno*, papal encyclical, Rome, 15 May 1931.

A Select Bibiography

—— *Lux veritatis*, papal encyclical, Rome, 25 December 1931.

Pius XII, *Sacra virginitas*, papal encyclical, Rome, 25 March 1954.

—— *Questa grand vostra advanta*, apostolic letter, Rome, 21 October 1945.

—— *Fulgens corona gloriae*, papal encyclical, Rome, 8 September 1953.

—— Address to young women of Catholic Action, Rome, 24 April 1943.

—— Address to women of Catholic Action, Rome, 26 October 1941.

—— Address to newlyweds, Rome, 25 February 1944.

—— Address to newlyweds, Rome, 8 April 1942.

—— Address to members of the congress of Italian association of Catholic midwives, Rome, 26 October 1951.

Ruether, R., & McLaughlin, E. (eds), *Women of Spirit*, New York: Simon and Schuster, 1979.

Ruether R., *To Change the World: Christology and Cultural Criticism*, New York: Crossroad, 1981.

—— *Sexism and God Talk*, Boston: Beacon Press, 1983.

—— *Woman Church*, San Francisco: Harper & Row, 1985.

—— *Mary: The Feminine Face of the Church*, Philadelphia: Westminster Press, 1988.

—— 'Religion and society: sacred canopy vs prophetic critique', in M. Ellis & D. Maduro (eds), *The Future of Liberation Theology*, Maryknoll, NY: Orbis, 1989.

Russell, L. (ed.), *Feminist Interpretations of the Bible*, Oxford: Basil Blackwell, 1985.

Schaberg, J., 'The foremothers and the mother of Jesus', *Concilium*, 206 (1990), pp. 112-119.

Schneiders, S., 'Women in the fourth gospel and the role of women in the contemporary church', *Biblical Theology Bulletin*, 12, 2 (1982), pp. 43-44.

—— *Women and the World*, Mahwah, NJ: Paulist Press, 1986.

Summerton, O., 'Pope John Paul on women,' *Vidyajyoti Journal of Theological Reflections*, 53 (1989), pp. 219-222.

Swidler L., *Biblical Affirmations of Women*, Philadelphia: The Westminster Press, 1979.

—— *Women in Judaism: The Status of Women in Formative Judaism*, Metcuchen: The Scarecrow Press, 1976.

Tetlow E., *Women and Ministry in the New Testament*, Mahwah, NJ: Paulist Press. 1980.

Van Lunen Chenu, M-T., 'Between the sexes and generations: maternity empowered', *Concilium*, 206 (1990), pp. 31-41.

Vanzan, P., '*Mulieris dignitatem*: reazioni, contenuiti e prospettive', *La Civilta Cattolica*, 139, no. 4, November 1988.

Vatican II, *Lumen gentium*, 'Dogmatic Constitution on the Church', Rome, 1964.

BELOVED DAUGHTERS

—— *Gaudium et spes*, 'Pastoral Constitution on the Church in the Modern World', Rome, 1965.

Von Balthasar, H., *New Elucidations*, San Francisco: Ignatius Press, 1986.

—— *The Glory of the Lord*, vol.1, Edinburgh: T&T Clark, 1982.

Wacker, M-T., 'God a mother?: on the meaning of a biblical God-symbol for feminist theology', *Concilium*, 206 (1990), pp. 103-111.

Wainwright, E., 'In search of the lost coin: toward a feminist biblical hermeneutic', *Pacifica*, 2 (1989), pp. 146-154.

Weildman J. (ed.), *Christian Feminism: Visions for a New Humanity*, San Francisco: Harper & Row, 1984.

Welch, J. (ed.), *Communities of Resistance and Solidarity: A Feminist Theology of Liberation*, Maryknoll, NY: Orbis, 1985.

Wilson-Kostner P., Faith, *Feminism and Christ*, Philadelphia: Fortress Press, 1983.

Worgul, G. S., 'Ritual, power, authority and riddles: the anthropology of Rome's Declaration on the Ordination of Women', *Louvain Studies*, 14 (1989), pp. 38-61.

Index of papal and church documents

JAN 3 1 2018

CPSIA information can be obtained
at www.ICGtesting.com
Printed in the USA
LVOW13s1605190118
563158LV00011B/511/P